D1133854

ÆSTHETIC ANALYSIS

ÆSTHETIC ANALYSIS

BY

D. W. PRALL

THOMAS Y. CROWELL COMPANY
NEW YORK

Apollo Edition, 1967

PREFACE

I wish here to express my gratitude to the friends who have given me so much help with this book. Without their suggestions and their criticism, it could not have been written. Although the ideas in it seem to me important and relevant, I realize that much of the subject matter considered is not regularly expected in a book on æsthetics. The discussions amount to theoretical spadework; they do not pretend to be a systematic survey of the field; much less do they constitute a general account of the arts.

I am most of all indebted for critical suggestions to Professor Ralph W. Church and Dr. Henry S. Leonard. The manuscript was also read, very greatly to its advantage, by Professor W. R. Dennes, Dr. Frederick Bracher, Mr. John R. Reid, Miss Isabel Creed, and by my sister, without whose aid I should not have attempted either the account of the musical scale here given or the account of the temporal patterns of verse. The proof was read by Mr. Oscar H. Shaftel and Mr. H. M. Austin, and Mr. Austin prepared the index.

D. W. P.

Leverett House,
Harvard University,
Cambridge, Massachusetts,
March 20, 1936

TABLE OF CONTENTS

INTRODUCTION

It is common to assume nowadays that what constitutes æsthetics or "the æsthetic approach" is necessarily dilettante in orientation. The assumption is supported, of course, by the typical speculation—vague in reference, grandiose in claims—that is conjured up by any mention of the subject. Whether speculation of this order serves a purpose can best be determined by those engaged in interpreting experience and behavior in general. There is little doubt that it is insufficiently concerned with the unique experience of what I should like to call, without invoking Platonic essences, the work of art *qua* art. Indeed, the preoccupation of æsthetics with issues that seem not to be relevant prompted J. A. Passmore a few years ago to suggest that we have been victims of an "attempt to construct a subject where there isn't one." The essay in which he did so sported the provocative title "The Dreariness of Aesthetics," and was heartily welcomed for its frank articulation of an attitude many of us secretly shared. It urged us to declare a moratorium on all generalizations about "art," and to devote ourselves to "an intensive study of the separate arts," giving emphasis to "real differences between the works of art themselves."

In an important sense, just such a study was advocated by *Aesthetic Analysis* when it appeared in 1936. For those of us striving for a better understanding of art and finding ourselves instead confronted again and again by still another æsthetic theory, it was an immensely sobering experience. It seems remarkable that after all these years Prall's example should have had so little effect, and that people should be still clamoring for a return to a direct and realistic approach. Perhaps one of the reasons for this is the tendency to read Prall in conformance with our received ways of reading treatises on æsthetics. Thus, when he acknowledges an "æsthetic experience," we take it for granted that the object of his book is the analysis of some generalized experience of this sort and not of art. When we then encounter his concept of "æsthetic surface," we are reassured that such must be the case. Surface, capitalized and perhaps italicized, now joins the impressive list of transcendentals that purport to tell us what art is but merely beg the question elaborately: beauty, myth, intuition, significant form, etc. Whether we accept or reject Prall hinges on how we feel about the philosophic basis that we think surface entails.

Surface is not of this nature at all, as I shall attempt to show later. What it entails is a direct and realistic approach to works of art. If I had to account for the fact that it was not primarily the philosophers but practicing artists and critics who rallied around Prall in the 1930's at Harvard, where he was a member of the philosophy department, I would stress this direct and realistic approach that puts one in the way of apprehending art better and understanding it for what it *is* rather than in terms of what it can do. What art can "do" is a concern that leads us away from works of art since often other things can do the same. This concern makes us ask such questions as, What cosmic significance does art have (art as "spilt" religion, etc.)? How does it afford the artist an outlet for self-expression (getting rid of aggressions, sublimating the Oedipal drives)? How does it afford the audience an outlet for relaxation or escape (when LSD or a warm bath are not available)?

Prall was well aware of the impossibility of one person setting himself up as authority on several arts. Instead of presuming to undertake their study himself, he was content in *Aesthetic Analysis* to broadly suggest the directions such study should take. But he had an unusually wide and intimate acquaintance with the products of all the arts. He was strongest, I suspect, in the visual arts, and he surrounded himself with choice paintings in his apartment at Harvard's Leverett House, which he occupied in his capacity of Senior Tutor (I recall, in particular, the portrait of him by Tchelitchew). Musical technique being the specialized affair that it is, I trust I do not sound patronizing if, on the basis of my participation in his student circle as a composer, I simply say that his knowledge of music and its mechanics was much more than ample for his purposes. (It helped that his sister, Margaret Prall, was a musicologist.) As for literature—poetry, in particular—significance may be attached to the esteem in which he was held by his devoted young colleague, the literary critic F. O. Matthiessen—himself in turn the center of an admiring circle that intersected with Prall's.

Among the students in Prall's circle of those years, there are three I should like to mention here since they went on to success in music, painting, and poetry: Leonard Bernstein, Robert Motherwell, and the late Delmore Schwartz. For them, as for the rest of us, what inspired confidence in Prall's eminently sensible views on art was not the information about art that he had amassed, but his taste and sensitivity. There is no ideal member of the artist's audience, but Prall approached very close to the status of being one. In his last years he seemed to accept this more and more as his role, and in this connection I am indebted to Henry D. Aiken (currently of the Brandeis philosophy department) for reminding me of Prall's increasing reluctance to style himself a philosopher, coupled with a cynicism about philosophy itself. It is hard to know from this distance how much this cynicism was simply the disenchantment that ultimately descends on most of us with regard to the crassly professional aspects of our profession. But a significant change was taking place, and it had started during the writing of *Aesthetic Analysis,* where we encounter the following surprising declaration on the very first page: "Thus it will be no reproach, and will do our study no damage, if what we attempt to make out as æsthetics comes to be better named in the future."

What a pity that our positivistic music theorists who have recently emerged on the American scene would not embarrass themselves with any book bearing in its title the word "æsthetics," even to the extent of flipping it open to its first page. A sentence such as the above might give them pause, and they might be still more intrigued when Prall later speculates on æsthetics as a science—making it quite clear, however, that it is not natural science that is in question, but something closer to what Baumgarten, the founder of æsthetics, had in mind. (Baumgarten is not mentioned, but the phrase "the science of the immediate" may be traced to that source.)

It is intriguing to speculate over what might have developed out of the unusual trend of Prall's thoughts in his last years had his life not been lamentably cut short in 1940 when he was fifty-four. There is every reason to believe that a third book would have surpassed *Aesthetic Analysis* in the crystallization of an autonomous theory in the same proportion that this second book surpassed his first one, *Aesthetic Judgment* (1929). In *Aesthetic Judgment* Prall was still much concerned with his predecessors—Croce and Santayana, in particular. The only sources that are acknowledged to any extent in *Aesthetic Analysis* are Birkhoff's *Aesthetic Measure* and Dewey's *Art as Experience*. These sources interested him only at the level of primitive assumptions. He did not follow them through to the conclusions about art that either of them proposed.

Birkhoff's idea of putting numerical values on spatial and temporal patterns, tonal harmonies, etc., was considered decidedly offbeat in its day, though lately information theory and computer analysis lend a certain stylishness to this kind of approach. Prall was not attracted by the idea of making value judgments with Birkhoff's numbers. What did attract him was the precise assessment of structural similitude and differentiation, for he was appalled at "how loose and confused and misrepresentative are such terms as *balance* and *symmetry* as so generally employed by æstheticians and critics" (page 87). Whereas Birkhoff was useful to Prall in coping with structure, Dewey threw considerable light on the expressive aspect of art. I realize that in some circles it is the nadir of naïveté to maintain that art embodies or communicates feeling. "I consider music by its very essence," Stravinsky declared in 1935, "powerless to express anything whatsoever: a sentiment, a phenomenon of nature, or the like . . . ." Needless to say, coming from a towering master, this statement has been enormously influential. Since my admiration for Stravinsky is unbounded,

I was very much relieved when he recently qualified it in one of his books of conversations with Robert Craft, *Expositions and Developments* (page 114):

That overpublicised bit about expression (or nonexpression) was simply a way of saying that music is suprapersonal and suprareal and as such beyond verbal meanings and verbal descriptions. It was aimed against the notion that a piece of music is in reality a transcendental idea "expressed in terms of" music . . . It was offhand and annoyingly incomplete. . . . music expresses itself.

As far as Prall is concerned, the way in which Dewey helps clear up the recalcitrant matter of expression is by reminding us how some experiences stand apart from the flux of experience by virtue of being their own fulfillment. The distinction between experience in flux and what Dewey calls "*an* experience" is that in the one case there is "distraction and dispersion"—we "put our hand to the plow and turn back; we start and then we stop"—whereas in the other case we have reason to rest content in the present moment, and both our interest and attention are fixed on the immediate rather than upon something that is liable to happen later. Although Dewey is discussing more than art, he helps us toward a clearer understanding of how the form or structure of a work of art is not merely some receptacle into which the artist deposits content, feeling, meaning—or whatever is your terminological preference. What occurs, rather, is that the experience itself (the content, feeling, meaning, etc.) assumes a certain arrangement that renders it, when it comes to its conclusion, "a consummation" rather than just "a close." To designate the "arrangement" as the form, as we shall see, does not render it something separate in the sense that a receptacle is separate. This degree of identification between form and feeling departs quite noticeably from Santayana, because even if his form as "first term" and feeling as "second term" are invested with equal status, the separation leaves room for a precarious upsetting of the balance that could lead to the following absurd conclusion of a philosopher of music of the 1920's: ". . . the appeal of music is to the feelings, and only to the feelings . . . . The intellectual factors in a work of art are only merits insofar as they are facilities bridging the gulf to the feelings."

A trivial but bothersome complication that contributes to the dualistic theory is the linguistic ambiguity that makes some people think of form as the conventional pattern whose bare outlines and minimum requirements you can find in a lexicon or handbook: *viz.*, sonnet form, sonata form, etc. This is why there is a preference for the term "structure" when more significant formal attributes or the total relations are in question. And yet I think it is a good idea to continue using the word "form" in its traditional generic sense—if only to keep reminding ourselves that any statement made about works of art, about either their form or their feeling, is necessarily limited and, in a sense, incomplete. The statement, "This work is in sonata form," tells us very little more about a work than the statement, "The *Pathétique* Sonata is in C minor." Every sonata is unique, and every work in a given key is in that key in a different way.

These things are so palpable you may wonder why I bother saying them. The reason is there is a moral I hope to draw. If it is granted that the conventional form—a sonata, for example—is not a receptacle for the totality of

notes or the feeling or whatever you please; if it is granted
that in the concrete sonata this conventional form becomes
a superficial aspect of the total form and becomes intimately
identified with the latter; if it is granted, further, that the
conventional form is recognizable in the totality by virtue
of the fact that we are capable of abstracting and thinking
about the superficial layer that constitutes the minimum requirements of sonata form, then it might also be understood
how, in some loosely analogous way, the feeling becomes
identified with—becomes, so to speak, lost in—the form.
That we have been able to talk intelligibly for so long about
a dualism between form and feeling, or the presence of
one and the absence of the other, is due to our capacity for
abstraction. But we have not always been clear about what
has been abstracted, and we have often mistaken the abstraction for the concrete object itself—for example, when
we have taken Beethoven's sonata to be the sonata form in
the book.

In short, it is only in the realm of discourse and thought
about art, the realm of analysis, that we can talk about the
form without talking about the feeling. Yet even this can be
deceptive, since every statement about the form is indirectly
or obliquely a statement about the feeling. "The *Pathétique*
Sonata is in C minor" is, as I have said, a superficial statement about the form. It is pretty vague. "The slow intro-
duction of the *Pathétique* Sonata is brooding" is a superficial statement about the feeling. It is also very vague, but
somehow we find its vagueness much more objectionable
than the specification of the mode and key. Now suppose I
make just a few little formal changes—canceling out some
of the flats—so that the statement about the form must
now be "the *Pathétique* Sonata is in *C major*." However

vague the statement about the feeling was, the word "brooding" is no longer apposite. In changing the form, I have changed the feeling.

There is, of course, something highly fatuous, useless, and inordinately unmethodical about these qualitative adjectives for characterizing feeling. This is why we favor more precise vocabulary and methods for dealing with music in terms of the form. The point was put very well some years ago by a fine musician who was also an Aristotelean—Herbert Schwartz by name. Whether we describe or analyze our listening experience, he said, "as the formal relations of a composition, or in terms of our feeling, we are talking about the same thing. The form is felt and the feeling is formal, and that is the he and the she of it. The 'he,' however, is somewhat more articulate." He still had hopes of arriving at a rigorous language for approaching music from the point of view of its feeling. Prall, however, who is absolutely brilliant in his treatment of the nature of abstraction in analysis, is reconciled to concentrating his efforts on the language available for stipulating the form. He also puts the matter very well, but rather late in his exposition (page 152 f.), where some of his readers, depending upon the camp in which they have settled, may have already abandoned him as being either a formalist of the "Art for Art's Sake" persuasion, because he dwells so much on structural relations, or an eminently unsophisticated sentimentalist, because he so much as deigns to mention feeling. He does not claim that we analyze the form to explain the feeling, but he is prepared for the contingency that some intelligent person may grant the vagueness of an epithet like "brooding" but still look for specifications as to the degree in which such a feeling is present. In formal analysis this has a certain analogy with looking for specifications as to the degree and manner in which a given piece is in C minor. If such specifications of feeling are sought, he tells us, "what could these possibly be but specifications of tempo, loudness, timbre, rhythm, pitch sequence, and so on"—in other words, specifications of the form.

If form and feeling have so often been regarded as two entities joined together, it is partly because we equate description, analysis, verbalizing, or conceptualizing of a work of art with our experience of the work of art itself. We are deluded into thinking that because we are obliged to talk about them with two different vocabularies they must indeed be separate. Here is where æsthetic surface plays a role to distinguish the work of art from the processes that bear upon it without being intrinsic to it. To avoid endlessly puzzling over how surface can constitute the essential experience of the work of art, we must guard against a conditioned response to conventional applications of the word that are not relevant here, e.g., "superficial" or "flat outer layer." There is no inscrutable immanence that descends upon surface to magically invest it with depth, with form as well as feeling. Any object at all, as a result of a shift of attention, reveals its surface to an observer. By maintaining this, Prall is relieved of the necessity to posit a special domain where only works of art exist. Such a domain, on which so many æsthetic theories are based, implies that only works that succeed, that are masterpieces, are admissible into it. If this is so, what is to be done about works that are rank failures, or even those that almost make the grade?

It is of the utmost importance to appreciate how much this sets Prall apart from other æstheticians and art theorists. For Prall, æsthetics is not concerned with beauty alone, and moreover—despite the title of the final chapter, "Critical Standards"—"æsthetics is not primarily concerned with value judgments" (page 179). The determining factor is the shift of attention to which I have already referred. It would be presumptuous of me to briefly paraphrase this subtle concept that Prall has delineated so well with many ramifications and qualifications. Let me simply say that it is a shift of attention that I might very well experience as I write these words at my desk. I have only to sit back and become aware of the desk's directly felt appearance (its surface). I contemplate it for itself rather than take it for granted as something—almost anything—that serves my purpose to write upon. It is a stark piece of furniture, not particularly prepossessing, and I become disturbed by the clutter of papers—not because they are letters to answer (this would carry me into discursive areas beyond the presented surface), but because they look bad. The thought that I must answer these letters may cross my mind at the same time. But as reasonable human beings we are capable, when we analyze our experience, of distinguishing between the direct and immediate apprehension of qualitative relations and our other preoccupations. Thus, "as no experience can be totally anæsthetic, so also no experience is totally æsthetic" (page 7).

Direct and immediate apprehension of æsthetic surface has suggestions of an obscurantist, Buddhist contemplation —an emptying of the mind. But this is to overlook the thoroughly intelligible manner in which knowledge becomes part of the surface. Let us suppose that in reading a poem you must consult a dictionary for the meaning of a word. You simply bring the meaning back and put it, so to speak, on the surface; and you need not make the trip again. Your concern now is with the precise way the meaning comes through the sensuous or musical aspect of the poem. T. S. Eliot once observed that "a poem may tend to realize itself first as a particular rhythm before it reaches expression in words." The concept of surface is simply a way of underlining a certain simultaneity in your experiencing of both the meanings and the sound.

Analyzing a piece of music may aid a listener to hear it better, and as preparation for better apprehension of presented surface, it is remotely analogous to making a side trip to the dictionary to look up a word in a poem. Since we leave the dictionary behind when we extract the word meaning, presumably we should dispense with the analysis when our apprehension is improved. But some professional musicians not only analyze music every time they listen, but they also seem to imply that there is one analysis for every piece, thus investing the analysis with the uniqueness and sanctity that the music itself possesses. This confusion of concept and percept is so prevalent among musicians that I was not surprised when a recent article in *The New York Times* complained about the propensity of our composers to make analysis an end in itself, while at the same time the author insisted that no one can "hear" a retrograde inversion. Now there are many musicians of my acquaintance who spend sleepless nights priming themselves to recognize retrograde inversions. But quite apart from this, after chastising composers for making analysis an end in itself, the author placed himself in a curious position when he said he could not "hear" an analysis. Hearing a retrograde inversion and hearing it *as* such (i.e., labeling or analyzing it) are two different things. (This is what I understand Witt-

genstein to be saying when he distinguishes between "seeing" and "seeing *as*.") This whole matter can be simplified
by an analogy with spatial relations. A certain shape may
literally recur in another part of the canvas, or it may recur
in such a way that it is reversed from left to right (retrograde), or turned right side up (inversion), or both reversed and turned right side up (retrograde inversion). But
whichever the case may be, a different kind of symmetry
will be achieved, and its effect will be accordingly different.
This will be true whether or not we have told ourselves
(verbalized or analyzed) how the effect was achieved. If
we fail to notice it, if our attention has not grasped the
symmetry, someone may help us do so by pointing it out.
In that case he will have to name it, using such words as
reversal, or retrograde, or inversion, etc. Returning to the
musical situation—the lamentable aspect of all this is that
many qualified and intelligent listeners are being alienated
from serial twelve-tone music because they are made to
feel that "hearing" a tone-row is naming the row and its
transformations, and doing so with a specific, fixed technical language. They would be less intimidated if they were
simply made to realize that "hearing" a twelve-tone series
is not the same as hearing it *as* a twelve-tone series—that is
to say, naming it and giving its structure. They need only
ask themselves whether, when listening to a Beethoven
quartet, they label the chords and key changes at every
point, or simply perceive specific differences which they do
not have the terminology to articulate. If the latter is the
case—which it most likely is—they can rid themselves of
all their qualms in approaching the new music, and proceed
to familiarize themselves with it in order to apprehend it
better.

One of the things Prall's surface accomplishes for us is to put these ancillary processes in their place (off the surface) without diminishing their importance. The book is naturally oriented towards analysis. At the same time, "Ideal æsthetic knowledge, absolutely ready response, would bury the whole system of discrimination in our nerves and our habits . . ." (page 57). Prall was not optimistic about anyone achieving this ideal, but he often talked about a "transaction" between the art lover and the æsthetic surface, his contention being that æsthetics should occupy itself with a transaction that was complete—one in which nothing obstructed the surface (such as the art lover's ignorance, inattention, or inadequate apprehension). He did not waste his time with the incapacities of the average or subnormal individual. It is reassuring to find that one of the most vital current intellectual movements, formal linguistics, takes the same stand:

Linguistic theory is concerned primarily with an ideal speaker-listener, in a completely homogeneous speech-community, who knows its language perfectly and is unaffected by such grammatically irrelevant conditions as memory limitations, distractions, shifts of attention and interest, and errors (random or characteristic) in applying his knowledge of the language in actual performance.

I trust that whatever analogy between music and language is implied by the above excerpt from Noam Chomsky's *Aspects of the Theory of Syntax* (page 3) is recognized as being harmless enough not to compromise me as contributing further to the abuses of treating the arts (especially music) as languages. To be sure, they have much in common: expression, communication, a disposition towards certain formal devices, etc. But they are fundamentally different—in some respects, even opposites. A systematized art theory based on a given style or technique —the theory of tonality, for example—might very well profit from being explored as a language. But music is not theory, though one gets the impression more and more these days that it is or ought to be—especially in university circles where composers seem impelled to justify their presence by giving music the stamp of scientific verifiability that theory can vouchsafe.

Having, I trust, sufficiently qualified any analogy between art and language, let me venture to suggest another potential parallelism between Prall and our current distinguished linguist, this one revolving upon the latter's growing confidence in the innate and the former's firm belief in our "readiness of response" to natural or native "concrete structural complexes" that are "peculiar to certain qualitative aspects of sensuous material." Whereas Prall is referring to materials (visual and auditory, spatial and temporal) and our given (including physiological) ways of perceiving them in a predetermined manner, Chomsky has in mind our capacity to develop our thinking along certain given lines, with the result that a plausible generative linguistic theory can offer "an explanation for the intuition of the native speaker on the basis of an empirical hypothesis concerning the innate predisposition of the child to develop a certain kind of theory to deal with the evidence presented to him" (*op. cit.,* page 25 f.).

The endorsement of innate capacities of any kind by some of our liveliest current thinkers is useful ammunition against the behaviorist, genetic, historical orientation that has so long pervaded our attitude towards the arts. Prall would have been the last person to deny that listening, say, to the corpus of Schoenberg's music enhances our apprehension of any given work of his. This does not mean, however, that when we hear this given work we must keep looking to the left and right of its surface where the other Schoenberg works are stored. Moreover, our enjoyment is obviously not the result of our having heard some other Schoenberg work yesterday. Since the relations have native intrinsic structures, our previous listening was simply to make us more alert to what is immediately given. By the same token, a composer may have special intentions, but he cannot legislate that the relations are anything he wants them to be. It is a good idea to avoid the habit of waiting for tonal resolutions when you listen to atonal music. But while a triad may have many associations as a result of its role in some two centuries of tonal music, it is not, as is so often assumed, tonal music that is mainly responsible for the quality it now has for us.

These assorted thoughts have been preliminary to facing the fundamental problem of Prall's natural intrinsic orders. It was probably by extension of musical theory that he developed it into a concept for all the arts, since virtually every harmony book starts with explicating the manner in which strings and columns of air vibrate not only in the whole, but in parts that stand in a regular arithmetic relation to one another. The unfortunate aspect of all this is that the significance of the overtone series has been so abused that many musicians and theorists—especially those in or inclined towards the avant garde—see red at its mere mention, and at any reference to the word "natural." Prall, who is, I fear, carried away by the neatness of this natural source and veers to the traditional line of music theory a bit too closely for comfort, is bound to be construed by musical readers as having committed what is sometimes known as the "naturalistic fallacy." The following passage from a recent harmony book represents it at its worst:

The major mode is a natural phenomenon and is always assumed when a single tone is heard. With the sustaining pedal depressed, play a low bass tone on the piano and stretch your ears to catch a chord quality. This simple experiment will prove tonality: two indisputable facts emerge. The irrepressible tones which sound most clearly are perfect fifths and major thirds, those which complete the major triad and imply the major tonal center.

Now the fact that is consistently overlooked—and Prall cannot be blamed for having followed musical theorists since Pythagoras in this—is that the harmonic overtone series (produced by the vibration of the partials in arithmetic progression) is *not* a necessary condition of tone. There are tones without any overtones at all ("pure" or "sinusoidal" tones) and other tones in which the partial vibrations do not stand in any such regular relation as an arithmetic progression (tuning forks, timpani, chimes, etc.). But even if there were only tones with harmonic overtones, why should the simple intervals produced by those overtones reign over the organization and movement of harmony like an absolute monarch? Perhaps I should say, rather, like an omnipresent God, since the privileged status bestowed on these intervals by medieval and Renaissance theorists had something to do with their capacity to reveal divine order. It may very well have been a survival of this belief that perpetuated them as the "good" intervals in later theorists like Rameau, Schenker, and Hindemith. This is equivalent to saying that because the right angle and the square are agents of divine or natural order, every painting must celebrate them. However, to do Prall justice, we should bear in mind that his preoccupation with the harmonic overtones was simply a means of demonstrating how nature provided a structural basis for composers to develop the major scale. Prall's way of extracting the scale from the overtones is not a hypothesis as to how it evolved historically. He is merely maintaining that its structure relies upon pre-existing relations, and it is not inconceivable that things might have turned out differently if other natural relations had been exploited. To be sure, there are simpler ways in which he could have demonstrated the scale's natural basis, and the reader who finds the technical convolutions too demanding for him can simply take cognizance of the general principle and proceed.

Though Prall has widened æsthetic experience to embrace more than just art, this does not contradict the claim I made at the outset that the main concern of *Aesthetic Analysis* is with works of art rather than æsthetic theory. The amount of space he devotes to the natural basic structures of the several arts is testimony enough, and I might add that as early as page 45 the exposition settles down to concrete matters when it takes up the serial order of pitches. By "serial order" he simply means the relation of pitches at discrete points in the continuum. But special interest attaches to his use of this terminology, since "serial" is an expression now consecrated to the techniques of the music that has been evolving since Schoenberg wrote his first twelve-tone works around 1925. Interest also attaches to Prall's use of the concepts of logic to explain his simple serial orders, since these very concepts are now used to explain techniques of serial composition by our most learned American theorists—and in such a way, moreover, that it almost seems as if they are subsumed by serial music alone, and not by any other music.

It is regrettable Prall used the word "sound" when he should have used "pitch" or "tone." (A sound can be a noise or a tone.) But despite this minor lapse, there is much to gain from the lucidity with which he handles the same logical concepts that are made to sound so frightfully obscure by our theorists of serial technique. In all fairness, however—and partly in admonition—it should be added that *Aesthetic Analysis* is not easy to read. Prall's elegant style is so concise and full of understatement, that there is real danger of extraordinary ideas appearing so casual as to pass unnoticed.

Arthur Berger

Brandeis University
Waltham, Massachusetts

CHAPTER I

THE FIELD OF ÆSTHETICS

I T WOULD seem fairly obvious that purposes not too clear to ourselves, more or less inarticulate tendencies, govern even our most disinterested attempts to know our world. And even *govern* is figurative; when the tendency has manifested itself plainly enough, we call the whole process by some name conveniently designating its apparent aim or nature. A general intellectual curiosity could not be exercised; exercising it would mean making it work at something, that is, become particular. But whatever makes it particular, unless our efforts are totally incoherent, will be what comes gradually to be organized as the subject matter that we are studying. Thus it is only an obvious condition of any study to a purpose that some so-called rationalization will label it conveniently. Later it may be more pertinently described in other terms; as theology, if it has any real subject matter at all, will some day no doubt be called after man or some part of what he experiences instead of after God. Thus it will be no reproach, and will do our study no damage, if what we attempt to make out as æsthetics comes to be better named in the future.

What *would* be unfortunate would be to find that our subject was nothing *but* a name. The only confidence that we can have in the value of æsthetic analysis, or for that

1

matter in any theory that is to be applicable to anything, rests on some clear point of reference to data that we can actually indicate. Pure science is so called because of the high degree of abstraction involved in it; the perfectly pure and totally inapplicable in any theory is emptiness or imaginative fiction, just as a perfectly pure intellectual motive would be *no* motive. For a motive has a degree of determinateness and in the end is properly named not by the imagined goal which its ignorance may identify as its intention, but by what it comes to accomplish.

At any rate the best name for any analytical study, however motivated, will be that of the objectively indicated field that it finally succeeds in systematizing. Its fruitfulness and relevance will depend on our starting out with some feeling, however inarticulate, for what is significant to us. This feeling will become articulate just so far as the analysis succeeds in bringing details together and thus delimiting and systematizing a single perspective. If the analysis is sound, it will give us a sense of genuine intimacy with what this perspective includes. It will be a map to help make us less strangers in one part of the world that we inhabit, less at a loss in the face of at least one aspect of what we experience. No longer merely experiencing it or being only vaguely aware of its content, we shall have some warrant for saying that we know it, that it is intelligible scientific subject matter.

It seems best, then, in an attempt to give an account of æsthetic analysis, to be clear as to the field that we are to survey. A further somewhat special reason for this is that æsthetics has been taken to deal with very different kinds of things. So many of these have been designated as its one proper subject that without this preliminary statement of intention any particular choice might appear unjustifiably arbitrary. Moreover, modern developments in the sciences, and more significantly modern studies in logic itself, have changed and clarified our ideas of what knowledge of a subject is, and how any sort of knowledge is systematized as a coherent body of theory. At first glance, then, our way of distinguishing the subject matter of æsthetics may seem not merely arbitrary in the way in which any definition is arbitrary, but, in the light of much traditional discussion, plainly misdirected.

It is not difficult, however, to illustrate the necessity for giving up some of the usual definitions of æsthetics if we are to preserve even the established meaning of the word as ordinarily understood. For one thing, æsthetics cannot be limited to investigating the concept of the beautiful. For there is meaning in the phrase *æsthetically unsatisfactory*. Beauty would be at most what is not æsthetically unsatisfactory. And illustrations are hardly needed to make it clear that we do regularly recognize the æsthetically objectionable, if we even distinguish æsthetic from practical or more strictly theoretical considerations. A wood fire may blaze brightly and warm a room comfortably and still be untidy, *viz.,* æsthetically unsatisfactory. Human beings regularly demand some degree of the ship-shape, their demand increasing in definiteness, though not at all necessarily in amount, directly with their intimacy with, and their practical interest in, the sort of thing involved. A cook demands a modicum of what seems to her a proper arrangement of her materials and her utensils in the kitchen. Plates are piled more or less neatly; the outsides of pots and pans are kept, if not as clean as the insides, at least cleaner than necessary for keeping food uncontaminated.

And although cooks do not always scour their pans on the bottom, they customarily recognize a degree of messiness that they find unsatisfactory just as a matter of appearances. But this is for æsthetic, not for thoroughly practical, reasons; it is not because a greater degree of untidiness would interfere with cooking. And so of writers and gardeners, librarians and pharmacists, cowboys and mountain climbers, tennis players and carpenters, mechanics and accountants. Æsthetically unsatisfactory is not a mere phrase, but a phrase clearly applicable, and not unfamiliarly applied, its meaning definitely known. Since beauty does not include the æsthetically unsatisfactory, it is plain enough that æsthetics, conventionally and regularly, usefully and soundly, covers a field of which beauty is only one limited, if infinitely important, part.

Still less is æsthetics solely concerned with what we conventionally call the fine arts. We have in the arts the æsthetically unsatisfactory and the æsthetically satisfactory; but both of these we have also in nature. And no one identifies art and nature. Art taken very broadly is just what is not nature, but is made or done by men; though it is natural enough, of course, in the sense in which men, and all that they are and do, are creations of nature and within her realm. But in this sense of the natural, there is nothing that is not nature. And art is acceptably distinguished as a level of activity or of product occurring only when men consciously and intentionally employ natural faculties and natural resources to ends they envisage, ends that nature can be said to envisage only so far as nature is embodied in one very special form, that of conscious human beings with wants and desires.

If, on grounds argued by some very great philosophers,

we refuse to admit genuine beauty in anything but the works of the human spirit, at least we need not rule out of the *æsthetically satisfying* all of the structures that nature alone is responsible for, mountains, forest trees, animal bodies—including us human animals—flower-forms and water and sky, sun and moon and stars. And if putre-faction and defecation are natural processes, their nature too offers to our nostrils some of the most strikingly offensive æsthetic content.

Not beauty only but also the æsthetically unsatisfactory; not the beauty or ugliness of the arts alone, but the whole panorama presented to us through our senses, the surface of our experienced world, is the field of the æsthetic.

But this appears to be the whole field of human expe-rience, the whole world as directly felt. It is simply the ex-ternal world, including our own bodies, inside and out, that begins to dawn on us in infancy, that offers to the most mature scientist exciting data for investigation, and to all men the only possible identification of the materials that they find and control, that they dominate, whether for use or for sheer exercise of power. Thus, instead of marking the limits of a field, we seem to have spread the æsthetic over all heaven and earth and their total content.

But this spreading will do no harm if in some other dimension we can mark a clear boundary line. The quali-tative presentation—and this is a redundancy; for all that is directly presented is quality—the qualitative presenta-tion of our world is just the æsthetic field. Not qualities recognized and tabulated and removed from their own felt mode of appearance, but qualities concretely had. Not a hue at no specific intensity, or a hue of specific intensity without spatial spread or temporal duration; but the red of this rose or of this structural steel of a bridge that is being built. The one is taken in by us as a determinate rich, fragrant, rose-red, the other as a hard, clear, red-lead red. Æsthetic surface is concretely had, directly and fully experienced. It is not merely distinguished by one of the senses, but felt emotionally in its full present character. But so far as it is æsthetic content, it is not *more* than thus directly felt. Once we go beyond into conceptual schemes, or into non-apparent physical constitution, we have penetrated the æsthetic surface; our activity has become intellectual. Cotton will suffice æsthetically for snow, provided that at our distance from it it appears snowy; for science this similarity is not even interesting. If we have recognized a shape as one fitted for a practical purpose, and our interest is no longer in realizing this shape fully but in using it to stop a hole or split a log, our attention being on a situation not here and now given through sense, but called up in relation to something that we want to do or to have somewhere else or at some other time or even presently—so soon as this is the emphatic aspect of our relation to any object, that relation is no longer one of æsthetic contemplation, and the object of it is just so far a practical object, not an æsthetic presentation.

It is the direction and, in the sense indicated, the depth of our interest, that makes the distinction clear; whether, that is, we penetrate the given surface to some ulterior purpose, practical or theoretical, or whether on the contrary we dwell directly upon its present nature as given. Practical or theoretical experience is directed upon data to serve further purposes, to go through or beyond the appearances to something not immediately appearing; æsthetic experience rests upon what immediately appears. To put it a little differently, the æsthetic aspect of experience is that in which, instead of employing the qualitative surface as a means and taking it for granted, we spend our whole attentive energy upon discriminating and realizing its full character as given. And it is plain that this aspect of our experienced world may range from being dominant, absorbing, and almost totally exclusive of any other aspect of the world, to being the merest passing sense of a qualitative presence, interesting only as fitting in with ideas and purposes directed through it to all that it may mean —beyond its surface—for the past or the future. It may fit into a conceptual content none of the rest of which is present, or be taken as the barest cue to activity directed far beyond what is present. Instead of discriminating and completely feeling the texture or the shape of a rock, we may recognize its convenient size and its smooth flatness and at once put our effort into making it skip on the water, or we may go off immediately into geological schemes and place it in a period. We may fit it into our knowledge of crystals and classify it. Or we may note its appearance accurately and swiftly, only to select it as a sample for analysis and because we think that an assay may show it to be valuable ore. In all of these cases it is not the world as æsthetic content that we are primarily concerned with, though such content is never totally absent.

One way, then, of marking off the æsthetic aspect of the world is as the world's immediately felt qualitative surface, in such small fractions of it as may appear to us. And we should of course remember that, as no experience can be totally anæsthetic, so also no experience is totally æsthetic. Even a young musical fanatic at a concert of his favorite music has some slight attention left for the comfort of his body and his posture, some vague sense of the direction of exits, a degree of attention most easily raised into prominence by any interference with his comfort by his neighbor's movements, or accidental noises coming from elsewhere, whether these indicate the danger of fire or some milder reason for taking action. Complete æsthetic absorption, strictly relevant to one object, is at least rare; the world as exclusively æsthetic surface is seldom if ever the sole object of our attention.

Mr. Dewey has made this out more clearly than any one else, perhaps. We must realize first that we live along in the infinitely complex processes that constitute bodily organic life within nature. We enter into all sorts of physical activities merely as a condition of being alive in the world. We respond to light and heat and pressure, taking up at the surface of our bodies all that they are susceptible of receiving. But we do not dissolve into natural processes. We are self-preserving nodes in the intricate and infinite matrix of natural flux. And only as we can, so to speak, condense process into quality, only as we can sum infinite minute perceptions into large clear ones; or, to speak more literally and in more modern terms, only as we become aware of felt qualitative content, are we even conscious. The æsthetic is what we experience directly and of necessity when we are not totally anæsthetized. Open to nature's surrounding variety of impinging activities of every sort, we are not liquefied or evaporated into the cosmic vortex. We resist in our own organic ways, and in so doing find a world, not ourselves, about us and present to us; present not as process itself, however, but as qualitative content. Mr. Dewey, in fact, calls this æsthetic surface the quality *of* the process.

He tells us that what differentiates the æsthetic is what marks off *an* experience from experience in general. As in the continuity of indifferent flux emotional tone is stirred and rises, it may, instead of merely falling again, remain for a little while determinate in what is objectively present to attention. Something qualitative is thus made out and raised from the stream of the indifferent and undifferentiated conscious or semi-conscious into what is distinguishable as a qualitatively individualized object. When the heightening is emphatic; when the aim of the experiencing activity is felt to be achieved in a vital process of receiving; when, to use Mr. Dewey's own terms, our doing has its own felt consummation, comes to its own realized fruition, not beyond the immediately present but in a direct undergoing, adequate and satisfying, then the æsthetic has taken on its distinctive character. This is immediate quality, directly felt as the unifying completion of the process of emotional perception. And to any conscious perception at all some degree of emotion is requisite, if it is no more than the excitement of the attention that brings it to a focus. The concrete object of æsthetic perception is just this determinate and emotionally intuited content.

Once we have taken definitely into account this unequivocally emotional character of directly intuited qualitative presentation, there is no great danger of misconception in marking off the æsthetic as simply the top level of all that is consciously experienced, the qualitative surface of all that we are acquainted with. For this in no wise deprives the æsthetic of richness or significance. So long as we keep to what is immediately present through our senses, remembering that the senses are not five distinct pieces of receiving apparatus, but many and complexly interconnected, and functioning only as instrumentalities of the integrated organism in a response involving emotional tone, so long are we experiencing the æsthetic aspect of things. How all this is related to beauty and the arts will become plain enough as we go on. And it is only as we find an adequate notion of the æsthetic in its broad scope in experience that we shall find the native place of beauty in our world, or come to any satisfactory, matter-of-fact account of the nature and the function of the arts.

But instead of marking off æsthetic data as distinguished from other data, or the characteristics that distinguish æsthetic experiencing from experiencing in general, it may make for clarity to distinguish æsthetics as theory from other theory, and particularly from those two sciences that are most likely to be confused with it, physics and psychology. For it is obvious that both physical and specifically psychological or physiological processes are conditions of the presence of the æsthetic. Without differences in external physical goings-on, vibrations of strings and air waves, or the reflecting surfaces of pictures, there would be no distinctions between one sound and another or one picture and another. And it is equally obvious that without correlative processes in our own organism, conditioning our conscious response, we should never find either pictures or music, not to mention differences among them. There is in fact some risk of mistaking a physical account of vibration rates for æsthetics itself. On the other hand psychologists are likely to claim æsthetics as one branch of their science, and æstheticians bent on realistic study are likely to speak as if they worked altogether within the limits of psychology. This would be cultivating an important field, no doubt; but it would be to neglect exactly the field that we have already been at pains to indicate as offering us the data of æsthetics proper.

An organism in nature, interacting within natural process, that is to say an unanæsthetized human being, is one of the conditions without which we never find æsthetic data at all. And an organism isolated totally from external physical influences would not only not have differentiated experienced content present to it; it would simply die. An isolated living organism is at most an incomplete image or an indeterminate conception. For organic life consists in being a particular organization of so much of natural process as centers at its center and moves in its specific mode of continuing to be. But æsthetic content is not process at all. It is quality; color and sound, not physical wave motions; it is attracting, exciting quality; deep, rich color, moving, emotional sound, not nerve currents or accelerated breathing or pulse. Æsthetics is not physics, then, nor psychology, nor yet physiology.

There is the physical organism and there are its physical surroundings. But æsthetics is not primarily interested in either of these. Its direct object is presented conscious content, objectively discriminable sensuous presentations. And the methods and technique of psychologists are no more useful in analysing the æsthetic aspect of our world than are the methods of physics. What all three sorts of theory have in common is that each is a species of analysis. The result of physical analysis is knowledge and control of physical processes, as the result of psychological analysis is the knowledge and control of psychological processes. Æsthetics seeks to know not processes at all, but a presented manifold, an immediately available content. While knowledge of this manifold may require, or lead to, knowledge *about* the æsthetic, its primary field is just this manifold itself, in its sensuous structural determinateness. All its results are correlations centering upon this, so far as they are not totally included within it.

But this is to say that æsthetics is the science of the immediate, and we shall at once be told that the science of the immediate is the very negation of science. For science has progressed by making hypotheses about physical forces and masses and substances and times, all measurable; hypotheses about insensible particles, or still earlier, about occult active agents or principles. And knowledge has grown clear and sure by avoiding qualitative descriptions and even qualitative terms, and turning to simple mechanical motions, to mathematical measurements, to equations showing the interrelations of such motions and such measures, until these relations themselves, as formulated in the equations, have come to be regarded as what constitutes the very essence and ideal of science, its basic and dependable laws.

But there has always been a feeling among philosophers, and still more strikingly among scientists who philosophize, that natural science has made a grave mistake whenever it has taken its methods as covering the whole field of possible theory and its results as our only reliable knowledge. There seems to be a natural impulse to deny the competence of scientific method in the humanities. History, we have been told, cannot be scientific, because every event is unique, just as every human individual is unique. One would even be led to suppose from this that historical events were not actual physical occurrences like other occurrences. Still more emphatically we are warned that scientific method is not applicable in any genuine study of the fundamental nature of morality or of beauty or truth, of the specifically human values most important to us. More than this: not even the field of the so-called secondary qualities—color, temperature, sound—submits directly to natural science. To study color we turn to measuring light; to study sound we count vibrations and trace wave forms. And none of this deals directly with the very material that we are acquainted with and wish to be more fully acquainted with. It deals instead with physical conditions, processes that condition the occurrence and the changes in sound or in color or in temperature, and give us control over the producing of specific sounds and colors and temperatures. Neither qualities nor values seem to be intrinsically amenable to natural science as we have it. If it were true that this is because science cannot deal with qualities and qualitative relations, the case might rest with the defeat of science at the borders of the humanities a foregone conclusion.

But we have been realizing during the last generation or so that the essence of science is not a materialism of particles of hardness; that what science has been actually formulating, where it has been most strikingly successful, is relations and abstract relational structures. Even the vaunted inductive method turns out to be ways of abstracting from concrete cases such clear and simple relations as can be put into relatively simple logical and mathematical form and viewed in these explicit connections. Mathematics is after all a complex development of logic itself;

and logic studies not merely the specifically "mathematical" relations, but any sort of systematic structure, the nature of which is capable of being discriminated as a complex of relations among elements. If, then, qualities have relations, and if these are systematic relations through which qualitative structures are grasped as intelligible complexes, qualitative wholes may also be amenable to scientific treatment. There is no reason why we should be confined to the sorts of relations that mechanics has depended upon for its triumphant progress and its effective application, provided that there are fundamental systematic relations of other sorts, or relations which are built upon principles as different from numbers and measures as a melody, for example, is different from a series of rates. If the melody is heard as a whole—clearly apprehended, that is, as some one determinate thing—it is to be expected that this heard melodic structure will depend for being thus apprehended upon our discriminating its constituent pitch relations. In fact, it is not quite an absurdity, though it is of course a dubious controversial point, to suppose that mathematics itself as used in the natural sciences has been limited by the nature of its foundations to relations abstracted mainly from extension, spatial and temporal. In the arts, where spatio-temporal relations are no more important than qualitative relations, or intuited geometrical relations (instead of strictly analytical mathematical ones), the foundations of intelligible structure may lie at least as significantly in such qualitative relations as in those of mathematics.

But whether this is so or not with respect to mathematics, it remains perfectly demonstrable—in the sense in which exhibition is demonstration—that qualitative relations, not numerical, not spatial and not temporal, can be discriminated as the basic structure of many aspects of the arts, and that training in discriminating these relations is the necessary condition of actual full acquaintance with works of art, and hence with the nature of art in general.

An example or two will suffice to illustrate this dependence of full acquaintance with an æsthetic surface or object upon the discriminating of such relations as are independent of the spatio-temporal and mathematical relations of the natural sciences.

To show that one kind of relation is independent of another, all that we need do is exhibit variation in a pattern constituted by this type of relation, while the pattern constituted by the other type of relation does not vary. To show that there are color structures distinct from spatial structures, we need only exhibit two different color structures which are spatially the same and which are themselves complexes of color relations. The difference between the two structures will thus be a difference solely in color design. Then we shall have to exhibit this color structure, which is independent of spatial structure, as itself constituted by strictly qualitative relations, relations intrinsic to the nature of colors themselves as distinct from their spatial spread.

We may suppose a flat disk, white in the center, which is surrounded by concentric bands first of light pink, then of rose-pink, and finally of full red at the outer edge. Without any change in this spatial arrangement of bands on a disk, we may substitute the outer red for the white center and reverse the order of colors in the bands, so that the outer edge of the disk is white. These two color designs are clearly different, not only strikingly in total

effect, but as analysed into the order of the color variations. The difference between the two is entirely a color
difference and dependent on a color relation. What, then,
constitutes this color structure as such? Clearly the exhibited color relations, the fact that there are all these degrees from white to red, distinctly related to one another
by the relation less-white-than in one direction, and less-
red-than in the other direction. If we could not depend
upon this perfectly fixed, intrinsically ordered variation
in color, we could not count on the variations to give the
specific effects intended. This ordered variation, where
the order is constituted by the single relation redder-than,
is only one of at least three systematic ways or dimensions
of color variation. But it must be clear from this one
sketchy example, where even our terms, such as *full red,*
are used without clear definition, that colors do lie in
ordered ranges, where we can speak of their qualitative distances from one another.

Out of this single relation no end of patterns could be
made. Say that we have only six variations from white to
red instead of the much larger number available. We may
number white 1, full red 6, and the intermediate variations, 2, 3, 4, and 5, in the direction white to red. Then
the permutations of these six variations are all color patterns varying not at all as spatial design, but giving to the
concrete colored area very different appearances with very
different effects, effects which have distinct emotional tone,
characteristic of the particular permutation used. Since for
every change in the relation of the variations there is a
change in the color pattern, it seems clear that the pattern
is constituted by the relations.

Any melody is an example of the dependence of structure upon native qualitative order in sensuous materials, a structure felt as having specific and even nameable character, only as the qualitative relation is grasped which is seen to constitute the native order intrinsic to the quality as such. The qualitative order of pitch is not the sole constituent of melodic structure, of course. But that it is one important aspect of it is fairly obvious. Say that we have a series of a dozen notes. We may decide on the duration of each, the tempo, the loudness, the timbre. But we may still make widely different tunes out of the notes by ordering the pitches variously. If, for example, there is a large pitch difference between the first and second notes, we say that one of them is far from the other in pitch and that the tune begins with a skip. But this would be impossible did not all pitches have each its own fixed place in a pitch order, an order intrinsic to musical sound simply because no musical sound lies outside this order, and because anything that lies in this order is a musical sound. Nothing that has pitch can fail to be a sound, and no sound fails to have a pitch. Colors and areas, lines and smells and tastes, do not possess pitch. Every musical sound does. We distinguish sound from noise by just this characteristic. And if sounds could not be relied on to have pitches, lying all of them at fixed points in the long line of pitch itself, there would be no way of following one sound by another in time and still having a distinct pitch interval between them. Thus it is the native order of pitch, every pitch being included once and once only in this one serial range, that accounts for the most characteristic feature of the patterns that we call melodies. And any one who fails to distinguish the basic relation, higher-in-pitch-than, or in the other direction, lower-in-pitch-than, fails necessarily to distinguish a melody so far as a melody is a pitch pattern.

If all this sounds like repeating over and over the obvious fact that colors and sounds vary in different ways, we need only turn to smells and tastes to find regions of sensory elements of which, though it is equally true that they vary, it is not true that they offer these variations in any order that we recognize directly and that would allow the sort of qualitative structure that we have been suggesting. For any two variations in color, for example, we can find a variation half way between, or a variation twice as far from one of them as from the other, along one of the serial ranges of color. And so of pitches. Pitches are at definitely apprehended distances *in pitch* from one another. And in music we have names for these measures of distance, the intervals, an octave, a fifth, a third, to take examples from our own scale system. How far, on the other hand, and in what dimension in taste, does the taste of pork lie from that of beans, or how far and in what direction or recognized dimension is the smell of violets from that of pine needles?

In the sensuous materials of color and sound we have not merely variation, but systematic variation; intrinsic, directly apprehended native orders from which the variations cannot be removed. In the order of hue, for example, red is far from green, and if we juxtapose red and green in a spatial area, they remain far apart in hue, and we feel this qualitative distance as what we call strong contrast. In sounds, if we follow C immediately with C an octave higher, or with G, the two notes refuse to be near together in pitch; and the result is a wide skip. There is no break in the temporal succession of sounds, but a definite skip in pitch itself, a skip actually heard as a big skip if we hear the pitch pattern at all, that is to say, if we hear the melody. Distinguishing this interval or pitch relation, or pitch distance, along with other relations of the same sort, is hearing the melody itself.

The objection that at once arises when æsthetics is put on this footing is that we have become formalists. And as every one knows, the formal abstractness of the elements and relations taken as fundamental is fatal to any grasp of the subject matter of æsthetics, if this is to include either sensuous content or emotional depth or human significance. But this objection has already been answered. For the elements we have so far suggested are not only sensuous but emotionally toned, and the structural relations are sensuous relations apprehended sensuously and with feeling. Thus we run no risk of formalizing the subject in such a way as to neglect the richness of its humanly significant content. When all of the sensuous elements are apprehended in just those relational structures which they constitute by virtue of the relations established in their native order, this grasp would not be the concrete apprehending of an æsthetic object, were it not the fact that such apprehension is in its very nature feeling. The feeling is strictly æsthetic, however, only if it is directed exclusively upon the object, so that it is properly the feeling of that object, not an irrelevance suggested by some incidental aspect of it, but a content determinately given as actually present to active contemplation. Such contemplation, in fact, removes irrelevant feeling just by being fully directed discriminating attention. Contemplation that does not attend and discriminate is either not æsthetic contemplation at all, or it is the æsthetic contemplation of something else, bodily states instead of the presented object, or remembered or imagined content not unambiguously determinate in the object. What is given to full, unwandering, vital response, without penetration through and beyond the qualitative felt presence defined by the object, is exactly the æsthetic aspect of the world at the moment. What penetrates and goes beyond is non-æsthetic.

But most response fails as æsthetic not so much because it goes beyond into other interests. Rather it goes beyond because it is not competent to apprehend the presented surface fully and determinately, and hence richly and excitingly. It is not full enough or discriminating enough to find in the immediately present content an adequately absorbing object. Any one who has ever been absorbed in looking at a tree in a picture has been occupied in discriminating lines, shapes, color variations, and just those shapes and variations that actually go together to make out this particular picture. Thus it is the picture itself that is exciting. And obviously this is not due to the fact that it is the picture of a tree. Recognizing so familiar an object as a tree is usually not exciting at all. It is only a tree that takes one's attention, a tree that occupies one's discriminating activity and absorbs one's feelings in its form and color, that is an adequate tree æsthetically. It may become individualized in its felt character as a strong, powerful tree, or a torn, broken tree, or a tree bathed in exciting light, or veiled in mist; but it is only a tree as fully realized and grasped in the concrete feeling of the given sensuous structure that becomes the object of complete æsthetic response. And for the most part we are too dominantly practical to train our perceptual discrimination to a point where such response is often appropriate or always possible.

That æsthetic response is for most of us on most occasions not possible is the great stumbling block. And this obstacle can be removed in one way and one way only, namely by learning perceptual discrimination. An example will make the point clearer. In one of Bach's three-part inventions, there is a passage which for our purposes may be given as the upward phrase *sol do re mi-flat*. This short passage has a certain gravity, partly because the succession is of notes of equal duration and not at a rapid rate. But after several occurrences in the invention, the phrase comes in again with one single change in pitch; the flatted *mi* is raised a half-step. The difference is in just this one interval from the next-to-last note to the last note. Only by hearing the two phrases do we come to appreciate, in their very pronounced difference, how much of the grave character of the phrase in its first form is due to our discriminating this last interval. There is a difference between the first and the last forms of the phrase comparable to the difference between the shape of a budding rose stem and the same stem when the top bud has opened into full flower, the difference between a milky spring sky and the same sky with one opening break of brilliant blue, the difference between a steady, sure pace forward on a stage with head bowed and a forward progress in which the last step is also the spreading of the arms and the raising of the face. The passage seems to me a good illustration, because any one not altogether tone-deaf can hear this difference both as the substitution of the different interval and as the total change in effect. Since all that comes through the ear in the two cases is the same except for the last pitch interval, it must be fairly clear that it is the distinguishing of a whole-step, where there was before a half-step, that is the very hearing of the melody itself in its full emotional effect.

Examples are not demonstrations. All that they show here is what is meant, in the cases suggested, by saying that æsthetic objects are structures dependent on relations, some of which are qualitative and not numerical or spatio-temporal. For any full grasp of the significance of such relations, whether in composing or in adequately appre-hending æsthetic objects, it will be necessary to give, abstractly and more or less systematically, an account of the basis of analysis here suggested as the foundation of æsthetic theory. This will occupy another chapter. But before beginning it, if we have defended or at least ex-hibited the relevance of such analysis, it is no doubt best to show at once how we avoid the more general con-demnation that such procedure always calls down upon itself.

This objection is variously put. It is essentially a belief —and a belief with a basis, of course—in the necessary falsification and the destructive character of analysis and abstraction. Because some abstractions have been mis-taken for the concrete actualities from which they were drawn, and because this has sometimes been done even by great thinkers, though much oftener by their too en-thusiastic followers, the actual abstractness of abstractions has come as disillusionment. Men studied certain aspects of human behavior in certain economic relations, and some men took this study to be a full account of men and life. Hence they were surprised—and the critics of economic theory were delighted—to find that the focus of these relations was not, as just this bare focal point, a concrete human being at all. The discovery was even taken to prove that economic theory was worthless because it was false to the humane nature of men, misleading as to the actual life of men together in society, degrading as an ideal of what a man may be. But no one, I suppose, seriously suggested that we wipe out the accumulated data, and *all* of the generalizations made upon it, and stop considering economic matters economically. And certainly every one would admit that economics has given us not only data, but generalizations actually useable in understanding and controlling a large group of extremely important social phenomena.

There are so-called philosophical arguments to demonstrate that a genuine *science* of society is an impossibility. But such arguments are simply neglected by men trying to gain knowledge about society. Their main virtue is, I think, to indicate that analysis and abstraction are confined always to fields limited by the very abstractions that constitute their foundations. We cannot know everything at once from every conceivable point of view. Quite obviously; for we always have, or are *at,* some *one* point of view, physically, emotionally, intellectually, and in every other way. All knowledge is from *some* point of view, and is guided not only by data found, but by interest confined to some data and not taking in other data. All knowledge neglects some things while it pays attention to other things. All attention is directed not only by some interest, but by means of some sort of conceptual scheme. It uses a limited number of terms and definitions; it comprises some single, though perhaps very spacious, perspective upon our world.

Knowledge must be relatively determinate in order to be knowledge at all. Omniscience is, if one stops to try and fathom its meaning, a hopelessly absurd notion, a logical impossibility. The lack of it is not a human limitation, unless knowledge itself is to be considered a human limitation. Being everywhere at once and seeing and understanding everything from every possible point of view, so that one's object is literally everything in all of its aspects and all its relations, would apparently involve being completely identical with everything at once. But being identical with anything is meaningless, except as it involves not being identical with other things. It is a fact, for example, that men feel differently about things. Omniscience would have to grasp all these different feelings, and all at once, so as to see exactly how one differed from every other; it would have to be at once exclusive and inclusive of everything not its particular chosen embodiment. The term simply refuses to take on meaning. An omniscient God would be his world in every particle and aspect of it, and so no longer God knowing his world at all. He would have lost his own identity, which requires his being distinct from other things. For actual knowledge, which is after all a human function, limitation is an obvious requisite. It is necessary, that is, to abstract from the concrete mass presented by nature's processes, some aspects of nature connected by some specific relations and thus capable of being viewed together. But this *is* abstract analysis; this is the way of scientific knowledge.

We must, in other words, if we are to have any knowledge at all, use the methods of abstraction and analysis. For we need to group elements together and to distinguish relations among them, if we are to apprehend any composite. And all works of art are composites. Æsthetic analysis is not itself æsthetic appreciation—much less is it artistic creation—any more than mechanics is riding in an automobile or inventing an airplane. But its relevance to both appreciation and to composition in the arts can be shown to be at least as obvious as that of mechanics to automobiling. The parallel is not altogether sound simply because æsthetics is æsthetics and not mechanics. What is peculiar to it is that its aim is intelligent acquaintance with the presented surface of the world instead of intelligent understanding and control of physical processes. What it does is to show the sorts of relations among sensory elements in virtue of which structures, sensuous and immediate, are apprehended and felt in their concreteness. But it can do this only by abstracting the elements and the fundamental relations first, and then exhibiting the structures as intelligible complexes of these elements in these relations. And it will be best no doubt, if what has been said so far is at all sensible, to be at some pains to be clear as to the basis of our analytical system and the logical form that would be its ideal consummation.

Such a consummation must, however, if there is anything at all in traditional notions of æsthetics, succeed in exhibiting familiar ideas and in including familar facts. It must make intelligible not only the so-called principles of æsthetic form, but also those most interesting cases of æsthetic objects, works of art. And it is only too easy to suggest at this point, as many theorists and teachers of art not only suggest but insist, that what we are most interested in in the whole range of æsthetic phenomena, even admitting that this range is as broad as we have been indicating, is art in its greatest manifestations. Why, we are asked, do we not start at once with masterpieces, and, if we must analyse and abstract, why do we not analyse these great examples?

The answer is pretty plain: such analysis comes at the end of æsthetic study, not at the beginning. In the first place, men are not quite agreed as to which are the undoubted masterpieces, though we might safely enough choose a long list. But if a great authority could omit El Greco from a comprehensive handbook on art published less than a generation ago, a book used very generally over the whole western civilized world, there is some caution to be exercised even here. And if we should look for a sure criterion of masterpieces, only sound æsthetics would serve to give us one. An æsthetics deduced from the study of masterpieces would justify whatever uncritical assumptions had been adopted in selecting them in the first place. The historical course of æsthetic theory would be against us too. For in such procedure from the top down, it has been emphasis on masterpieces that has led to the numberless esoteric criteria that have been adopted at various times only to be given up again. The basic criteria of beauty in art have changed along with changes in individual and social taste. An adequate æsthetics would not adopt these criteria, but find some explanation for their adoption, as it would also admit among its data the extreme relativism of taste itself. And all this on a much broader basis, on which the boundaries between æsthetics and other subjects might be clearer.

Moreover, those who are best acquainted with masterpieces in any one of the arts are only too likely to have so slight a grasp of the other arts as to neglect their fundamental nature or to read into them principles applicable only to that art in which they are experts or have achieved great scholarship. Instead of general principles, we are likely to get from them special principles, say, of painting. But what we are looking for are principles which should be just as significantly relevant to music or to architecture.

We must of course choose some data to abstract from and to analyse, before we can articulate the principles of this choice. But if æsthetics is one of the broad regions of human experience, and not an esoteric cult, then a selection of data under the common terms of conventional usage may be a better guide at the beginning than the knowledge of specialists, which is so seldom sound or wise outside its own range. And if it is the common experience of human beings that we are dealing with, then masterpieces as data are entirely out of the question. Not only are most of us not familiar enough with them to analyse them adequately, but only a scheme of analysis based on familiar general experience would even begin to show us the way to apprehending them at all in their actually experienceable character. There is something suspiciously incongruous in supposing at once that masterpieces are among the greatest achievements of the greatest minds and that a perfectly unprepared mind, usually of another generation—for masterpieces are always at least well on into middle age before they achieve their status —can, with a little attention, apprehend them in their full nature. It is a little as if one began mathematics by close attention to Einstein's equations—with a competent and appreciative mathematician as guide, of course—instead of first learning to count and add and multiply.

The parallel will be rejected only by those who do not realize that great creative art requires great intellectual powers. It is often supposed that great artists are not endowed with mind so much as with a spirit which directly externalizes itself, and that other human spirits, by virtue of their innate humanity, can grasp the spiritual essence thus mysteriously made available. But if so, then mere human knowledge, with all the training and development that it requires—except in the case of those special proclivities and abilities that are called genius—has no bearing on art at all, nor is æsthetics a subject for general study. Art is not solely an abstract intellectual achievement like mathematics; but to suppose that passion and spirit do not invoke intellect, and that great artists are not great minds, is a stupid blunder. It is just as stupid as to suppose that great mathematicians and scientists are not themselves moved by great passions or that they lack imagination. It is at least nearer to the apparent facts to say, as Hobbes did, that it is only great passions that animate any considerable intellectual activity, that "to have weak passions is dulness." At any rate, to those of us for whom the arts have come to have intelligible significance, so that there is any sureness in our grasp of them only after long and more or less arduous preparation—and for artists themselves the advance to control and accomplishment has not been free of slow struggle and development—it will seem only sane not to begin at the top but at the bottom. We shall even recognize the fact that in some of the arts we may never apprehend at all fully the great achievements, and that in those where we do, or think that we do, we have become capable of this grasp by virtue of wide familiarity with simpler things and long and detailed training in perception.

But the study of masterpieces has still more serious faults as a way to adequate æsthetics. Art is expression in a sense of the word that should become plain before we finish, and expression in art involves communication. But what is readily communicated is never the feelings and ideas of great men of other centuries, but the feelings and ideas of our contemporaries. And our contemporaries seldom seem to us great masters. What we may turn to masterpieces for is not to discover the nature of artistic expression, but the nature of greatness. And it is their greatness, not their mere æsthetic nature, that distinguishes great works, whether in the arts or not. Since any quick recognizing of masterpieces is obviously difficult except on the strength of authority, it must be fairly clear not only that we do not readily apprehend the individual character of works of art, but that when the best of them have been selected for us by others, their most distinctive aspect is not that they are works of art but that they are great. And though greatness is by definition infinitely important, no one, I suppose, would assert that it is a subject matter peculiar to æsthetics.

One other point must be made here as a caution. We have noticed the æsthetic significance of structure; when we do not grasp the sensuous structures of art, we do not apprehend the works of art themselves. But this is not to say that only those elements are æsthetic that are capable of conscious structural control by artists, and of apprehension as constituents of intelligible structures by other men. Only such elements as are capable of forming structural complexes can be made into such complexes; and only complexes of such elements can be intelligibly grasped as composed of these elements in their characteristic relations. But, as nothing is exhaustively intelligible to us in every part and aspect of its being, so there occur in the æsthetic aspect of our world all those natural sensuous elements that are not distinctly intelligible, though they are emphatically present and clearly discernible. Smells and tastes are obviously æsthetic, even though we do not—at least as yet—recognize their qualitative orders and relations in a way that allows us to use them structurally with any such degree of intelligibility as musicians use pitch and loudness, or painters, color values. The use of these sensuous elements, the qualitative orders of which are so much less clear to us than the orders of sound and color, is largely confined to enhancing other effects in art. In nature, however, these elements occur not only as such enhancing aspects, odor added to the form and color of a rose, but also alone. A sweet taste or a fresh smell is as definitely æsthetic as the rhythmic pattern of a dance or the complex sonorities of great music. And it is with sharp perception of such isolated elements that the æsthetic aspect of the world first comes to us, no doubt.

We do best, then, not to begin with masterpieces or even with the arts, but with the sensory materials that nature furnishes, some of which she has happily arrayed for us in distinguishably ordered manifolds, out of which the arts can make genuine structures acceptable to beings with passionately interested minds and discriminating perceptual faculties.

Æsthetics is a branch of knowledge; but it is knowledge of qualities in their immediacy and their immediately

grasped relations, directly apprehended in sensuous structures. It is made up of generalizations from data, as all
knowledge is. But its aim is intimacy with immediate
content at once sensuous and structural, readiness of grasp
in this broad qualitative field. Æsthetics will no more
teach us how to write poetry than how to build houses. But
it may teach us something of what it is that we hear in
music or see in buildings or enjoy in our own everyday
surroundings. It should inform us through abstraction and
analysis as to how the external world as immediate presentation is constituted, by nature itself or by artists, those
animate parts of nature who, with significant intent, have
been called nature's only legitimate children. And if we
wish to mark ourselves off as human and not merely
natural, it is as æsthetic beings that we are best characterized, beings capable of enjoying the æsthetic aspect of
the world, the world as we are directly acquainted with it.
And this at all the levels of experience, from bare conscious awareness of qualitative content as distinguishable
external presentation, to the intelligent grasp of great
works of art, where all the human faculties are exercised,
where perceptual discrimination and the intellectual understanding of complex relational structures, are fused in the
passionate realization of expressed feeling.

CHAPTER II

THE BASIS OF ÆSTHETIC ANALYSIS:
ELEMENTS AND ORDERS

B EFORE turning to the sort of analysis that constitutes
æsthetics, it may be best to have some approximate
notion of the nature as well as the function of abstraction
and analysis in general. For most of the objections to
analysis in a given field amount to saying that analysis
is limited to its own particular results, as if somehow it
ought not to be so limited. The objection arises largely
from not realizing either just what analysis is or what it
can do, what its limits are and what its aims. In the first
place we must remind ourselves explicitly that analysis is
not cutting things into pieces and destroying them. It
seems gratuitous to make such an observation; for analysis
is obviously a theoretical activity, an intellectual process.
But it has been so dinned into our ears that analysis de-
stroys instead of explaining, that we are likely to find ourselves believing this, though it could not conceivably be
the case. Even if the analysis is of nothing but a figment
of the imagination, and even if we become absorbed in
the analytical process and drop out of our mind for the
time being this figment of the imagination itself, it is
just as available as it was before, unless our memories fail
completely. To *it* nothing has happened. If it was ever
present, it cannot be done away with; and *explaining*

away is a misleading phrase for forgetting what we were
about or for concluding with what is irrelevant. If logical
analysis is applied to an actual physical object or to the
concrete quality had in an experience, the nature of that
object and of that qualitative presence remain what they
were, even though we may, with new light on them,
change our names for them. The strongest thoughts in the
world will not crush rocks nor move mountains; nor will
they destroy a government. If prayer, in faith, will do
these things, it is because faith carries prayer to a god,
himself supernatural, who yet has power to act upon nature at human suggestion, or because strong faith, having
emotional impetus in it, most naturally issues in literal
physical action.

Analysis may clear our mind sometimes of confusions,
as it may also force us to pay attention to one aspect of
things at a time, and so to drop other aspects out of
attention. But this involves neither destruction nor falsification. It does not involve destruction, because it is logical
process in us, not physical operation on things. It does not
involve falsification, because an explicit consideration of
one particular aspect of things in one particular way involves the explicit recognition that there are other aspects
of things as well as other ways of considering the same
things. An analyst may be more interested in the development of his own analysis—must be, if he analyses at all
—than in what at the time he is not analysing, not thinking about, that is. But the very nature of his procedure in
selecting his subject matter and his point of view to the
conscious exclusion of other subject matter and other points
of view, other foci for perspectives, offers the surest pro-
tection from falsification. Such exclusion definitely ac-

knowledges what is excluded without prejudice to its nature or to its actuality. And in definitely choosing one among many possible modes of procedure there is no criticism of other modes of procedure, but the clear indication of the fact that there *are* other modes.

Even in the case of the physical destruction of an organic compound to determine whether or not it contains suspected foreign substances, no one supposes that the finding of the latter involves the denial that the organic matter itself existed. An autopsy by means of which we detect poison in the stomach of a dead man is not taken to be the assertion that the dead man had nothing else in his stomach, much less that he had no stomach and no other organs. It is only by mistaking analysis for a complete description of literally everything all at once, and in all ways at once, that it appears as falsification.

The objection may still be raised that since any analysis omits at least something, as all actual thought is bound to do, it is therefore not the whole truth. But nothing is the whole truth. And it is only philosophers who identify truth itself with what they call the Whole, or such philosophical minds as deny the value of all detailed study that they are not interested in at the time, who can object to analysis as such in any given case. The objections of most other critics are answered by the simple reminder that all knowledge involves abstraction and analysis, that knowledge varies in relevance with the choice of what is abstracted, in scope with the magnitude of the field analysed, and in determinateness with the degree of systematic articulation achieved by the analytical procedure.

And there is no mystery about the sort of selection and omission—for that is what abstraction is—upon which analysis depends. We abstract elements simply by choosing details found in the object of our attention; these are abstracted from the rest of it. Moreover, there are distinguishable aspects of objects which cannot be concretely presented alone. What we call concrete objects are after all themselves of this sort in the end; but custom has cut them out for us as separate from their surroundings, without which actually they are unthinkable, since all things exist only in the matrix of nature. And much of the feeling against analysis is due to the fact that it does not follow custom in its choice of objects, but forces our attention into noting unfamiliar distinctions and boundaries. At any rate it is the non-separable but distinguishable aspects of objects that are thought of specifically as abstract and called abstractions; though we are likely to forget how familiarly we are acquainted with exactly this sort of thing in all of our thinking.

We do not find color separated from what is colored, and no one is worried by the abstractness of named varieties of color as such, though it is obvious that any definite color variation taken not as the surface of any object but just as the determinate shade that it is, is as abstract as anything could be. If we are to have an analytical account of the objects of vision we do not refrain from mentioning their color. Nor do we feel called upon every time that we do so, to remind ourselves or others that in speaking of the color we are not denying that it is spread over some area of the surface of an object. On the other hand, we do not mean by the color the spreading itself, the extension that is colored. In the concrete presented surface we simply distinguish the color from the extension, and then, if we are to consider this color, stop examining the extension or even mentioning it. We go even further. In color we distinguish hue from brightness, as in extension we distinguish breadth from length. No color is presented concretely without extension. No presented visual surface lacks two spatial dimensions, as no physical object lacks three. But it is not falsification to speak of the length without mentioning the breadth. And for the purposes of useful knowledge it may be only one of these aspects that we need to note. It is at any rate always at the expense of omitting some of them from consideration that we are able to attend carefully to any one of them.

That it is ten miles to the next town by way of the main road may on occasion be good solid knowledge, even if the road varies in width at every mile-post. Indeed, any one who should insist upon knowing the exact width of the road at every point before driving on, would only have begun his inquiries. For a road has not only length and breadth. It has roughness and smoothness, various grades of steepness; it is wet or dry, hard or soft; it is light or dark, and it may be dangerous or safe for a thousand different reasons, because it is much or little traveled, or because it runs along the edge of a steep cliff. So on indefinitely. In no case could our information about it include all of its characteristics. That would involve, among other matters, knowing its chemical composition at every point, the degrees of brightness of the sunlight falling on it through the trees at all times of the day and so on and on. It is not foolish to inquire only about such aspects of it as interest us, or to ask our informant for so rigorously abstract a single piece of information as its length. We should be extraordinarily unreasonable to call the information false because it abstracted from the infinitely various aspects of the actual road this bare abstract measure of distance. But obviously enough the length of a road is not separable from its actual being. It is just because we have abstracted for our purpose exactly what remains concretely a character of the road, and is *not* separated from it by our selecting it as a piece of analytical knowledge, that our abstract analysis, selecting only its length, is useful to us.

But it is only too plain that we may abstract the wrong features for any given purpose. If, in the case of the road, we wanted to complete mileage figures on a map, it might make no difference to us that a mile of it was three feet under water. But if our object was to reach the town at the other end, the presence of flood waters would be highly relevant.

Thus all analysis runs risks. Gaining knowledge is an experimental venture, not a dream, nor a logical demonstration. And if we are to get knowledge in the field that we have suggested as that of æsthetics, we shall have to venture upon abstracting elements from experience that seem to us to the purpose, and upon discriminating such relations among elements as appear to us to be relevant to the actual nature of the æsthetic objects that we know. But when we have finished we cannot reasonably expect to have found out all that there is to know about *anything*. Nor should we be sensible to hesitate on that account. It would be like hesitating to turn on the electric light because we do not know whether the house has been robbed in our absence. The way to find out is to investigate, and to do that we must begin to investigate and begin somewhere and somehow. Turning on the light in the hall may even be more sensible than finding our way in the dark directly to the bureau drawers in the bedrooms, a procedure much like that of an æsthetician who should begin his study by examining the pure beauty of the Italian primitives in a convent outside Siena. It is of course such extraordinary beauty that interests us most in the end, just as our interest in the money in the top bureau drawer may be all that instigates a search of the house. But a good light on the subject may be better than much fumbling in the dark, especially if in our fumbling we refuse to take note of anything but our final object. We must find the bedroom before we find the bureau; we must notice that the bureau has been moved to the other side of the room by the house-keeper in our absence, and we must have the key to the drawer, which turns out to have been laid on the shelf in the hall.

If this seems a banal and far fetched parallel, still it may suggest that any investigation, even one that is interested in high and complex objects, may do best by beginning with what seems very low and very simple, and at a very great distance from the final object of our greatest interest. If in æsthetics the objects of our investigation are genuinely structural, really composed, then it seems reasonable to begin with a survey of the elements that make them up, the structural relations native or possible to these elements, and thus the abstract analytical base upon which any knowledge of them, any full acquaintance with their nature, any direct apprehension of their individual quality, rests.

That in establishing this basis we do well to take as elements units of sensuous content is perhaps plain enough. But æsthetics has too often neglected those very aspects of this content that constitute the characteristic nature of æsthetic structures that are works of art, though of course artists and technical teachers of the arts have not been so neglectful. Although pitch is only one aspect of sound, musicians have long composed and taught very largely within one particular scheme of pitch intervals; musical analysis so-called refers entirely to this abstract scheme. This does not make musicians neglect rhythm or the timbres of instruments or differences in loudness and softness. But what musical notation indicates, so far as it indicates pitch, is an abstract aspect of sound. Pitch without a degree of loudness, without a given timbre, without some determinate duration in time, is not a concrete actuality. But if we are to deal with sounds in music, whether to compose or merely to hear a simple melody, we must grasp pitch relations.

The grasp of them at the minimum appears to be perception, not conceptual understanding. But the difference between perceiving clearly and understanding distinctly is not the great difference that we are sometimes led to think it. And the most obvious fact about knowing works of art is that direct apprehension is the final adequate knowledge that we want. So in æsthetics itself. Its final aim is the body of knowledge that conditions direct and adequate apprehension, makes us at home among æsthetic objects. But such apprehension in any particular case depends upon a readiness to discriminate sensuous details. What we need then is a systematic scheme that will put us in a position to grasp these details in particular cases and as constituting particular æsthetic objects. We need here what we need in all knowledge, the abstraction of such elements as can be ordered conceptually as kinds or groups. And when we group kinds, and our knowledge is no longer of particular elements merely, we have generalized. The form of our generalizations in systematic connection is an analytical scheme. And it would be impossible to generalize were not the particular elements so related, in definitely indicated ways, that our scheme of them may represent the discerned order of their actual nature and therefore be directed upon their actual ways of entering into structures as constituents.

This is assuming two points about knowledge that we have not so far explicitly mentioned and that cannot be much more than barely indicated here. In knowledge, as applied, the conceptual schemes that we are said to know are in the ideal case no longer consciously present. They have disappeared into physiological structures and habits of action. The expert, whether in mechanical operations or in mathematical investigations, can not keep his knowledge present in conscious content. He *feels* his way, and perfectly surely, whether with gears and keys or with the symbols of equations. He drives on through his material, just as a man walks from his desk to the door, with the very minimum of conscious conceptual content. But unless he has gone through such processes actually and repeatedly, and has put them safely away as dependable and almost unconscious habitual modes of response, he will not be an expert at all. If he loses his expertness, the only method of recovering it is renewed conscious attention to the scheme in which things have their places for him. Knowledge and expertness are one and the same thing. While both are gained characteristically by the struggle with content consciously present, both reach their consummation in the expert smoothness of direct action with a minimum of conscious content. In this sense, and to this degree, knowing is process or activity, and the knowledge that we are said to possess is embodied in the readiness to respond in certain fields in certain ways, whether these are called practical or theoretical, the fields of doing or of knowing.

The other assumption is not so easy to state briefly. It is simply that any conscious content is taken to be intelligible just so far as it is grasped as form or structure. This means, of course, as made up of elements in relations by virtue of which they actually come together. We see a situation as having a certain form, and we do not need to analyse that form into elements in relations provided it is simple enough to be grasped directly; familiar enough, that is, to be acceptable as it stands all together. But any scheme, any formal structure, whether a sequence of habitual conscious or unconscious acts, or a presented geometrical design, can be one only by virtue of some sort of coherence. And structures are grasped as such only when we are already familiar with them as wholes or types, or with their kinds of elements and the kinds of relations native or possible to these elements in complexes. For elements not natively ordered by a relation of some sort will not make structures for us at all, nor will intrinsically related elements make structures for us unless we have become aware of the kinds of relation involved. You cannot make a spatial whole except with elements the very nature and being of which is spatial extension. You cannot make melodic structures except out of elements which are natively ordered by an intrinsic relation in pitch from which they cannot be removed. This is to say not only that elements have character of some sort, in order to be elements of any one kind, but further that the character necessary to elements if they are to compose structures apprehensible as such, is relational character. The elements must lie in an order native to their very being, an order grasped by us as constituted by a relation. We call structures intelligible and feel that we know them in so far as we find them capable of analysis into such elements so related; and we should not recognize them at once as intelligible, recognize them at all, that is, were we not already familiar with these structural possibilities in the relations intrinsic to the elements.

We have already illustrated this in pointing out the condition under which two successive notes in music present us with a musical interval, and two color variations side by side in space with a color contrast. But we shall need to see more specifically and more fully just how such elements are natively ordered by certain abstract aspects of their own qualitative nature. And in doing so we shall be outlining the analytical base of systematic æsthetics.

As we have already suggested, and as any one surveying the field would probably agree, the elements that we are to take as basic should be sensuous elements, and the relations, since they must connect such elements, will be the only sort of relations capable of connecting sensuous elements, namely sensuous relations. It will be clear too that both the elements and the relations are abstract, that is, distinguishable aspects of the concrete sensory content, but not experienced separately from it. Some degree of abstraction is obviously necessary to any distinct experience of anything. We do not apprehend everything at once; we select the objects of our attention, as our organic processes select those physical influences that can be exercised upon them without destroying them. Just how far abstraction is to go is partly a matter of convenience, partly a matter of common sense distinctions, partly a matter of the conventional definitions of the sciences. For example, sound has been analysed by physics. The relevance of certain aspects of this analysis to musical sound is familiar. But it is equally plain that physics is not æsthetics, even when physics gives us pitch relations in terms of vibration rates, or color relations in terms of wave lengths. We come to the elements of æsthetics proper only when we treat sound as quality heard and color as quality seen. Thus our elements, if they are to be the basis of æsthetics, should be qualitative content, whatever the degree of their abstractness, not physical measurements.

The relevance of nervous process to emotional perception is equally striking; but æsthetics is not psychology, whether physiological or behavioristic. For psychological analysis is not of the qualitative field as presented but of its conditions in organic response. The correlation is plain, as is also the correlation to physical conditions. But what we have to find is analytic relations and elements in the actually presented content. Only so shall we have made out the distinctly æsthetic field. But it will be no disadvantage to our knowledge in general that the distinction between this field and that of physics on the one hand and of psychology on the other will not be a mere otherness but the boundary line of adjacent territory, the passage across being no greater, from the point of view of knowledge in general, than the passage across such a convenient line of demarcation as makes one slope of a mountain Spain while the other is France. The modes of travel may be the same on both slopes; the language has changed. And it is language itself, terms and relations in a systematic scheme, that constitutes and characterizes every field of knowledge in its explicit formal aspect.

Hence our question comes to be: What is the language of æsthetics? What are its nouns or terms? What are their adjectives or relations? If it is admitted that nature and the arts give us concrete structural complexes, and that æsthetic understanding is grasping the nature of these, as constituted of sensory elements in relation, then we must abstract such aspects of quality as are clearly relational, and survey the elements in the orders constituted by such relations. And since we have already seen that these relations are peculiar to certain qualitative aspects of sensuous material, we shall not expect to find them limited to the spatial or the temporal merely. What is characteristic of color contrasts is not only that they are spatially exhibited, but that the colors as such really do contrast, really are far apart in some aspect of color as such. And since this is not so obviously the case with tastes and smells and other sorts of sensory content like the feeling of muscular strain or of rhythmic pulse, we shall turn our attention at first to sound and color to see what we can discover in them that will explain, *viz.*, make intelligible, the structures of music and painting.

What we do find are non-numerical, non-spatial, non-temporal serial relations constituting serial orders. But the situation is complicated by the fact that these serial orders are not of the concrete sounds, not of hearable notes nor of concrete visible colors as such, but of aspects of these which are conveniently called dimensions on the analogy to spatial dimensions. As a geometrical structure may vary in length while it remains the same in breadth, so sound can vary in pitch while it remains the same in loudness, or *vice versa*. It is such independent variation that establishes the grouping of elements or terms in all analysis, and in our case a grouping in serial orders.

A relation constituting a serial order has certain properties. If it applies to a group of elements, then every one of these elements is related to every other by this same relation. This is called the connexity of the relation. A relation is said to have connexity when between any two elements of the field whatever this relation holds. Now all sounds have pitch, and every distinct pitch is either above or below any other pitch that we may choose. Thus all sounds are related in a single order, every sound to every other sound. We might simply say that sounds are pitch-related. But the point of a serial relation is that the sense of the relation, its direction, is part of what gives it its special character. Instead of being reversible or symmetrical, above-in-pitch is asymmetrical. A relation is called asymmetrical when, if it is the relation of, say, x to y, it can not be the relation of y to x. Thus if it is the fact that x is taller than y, this involves the fact that y is not taller than x, but shorter. If B is higher in pitch than A, A cannot be higher in pitch than B. If this seems too obvious to notice, we need only call attention to such a series as that of selected points on the surface of the earth. Chicago is related to New York by the relation west-of. And it seems at first obvious that New York can not be related to Chicago by this same relation, but only by its converse, east-of. But if we go east from New York to Southampton and Gibraltar and Singapore and San Francisco, and keep on going east through Omaha, we shall get to Chicago by a route on which New York is west and not east of Chicago. The series of pitches is not like this. It runs out in both directions instead of coming back upon itself.

The relation higher-in-pitch-than has a further property, called transitiveness. If B is higher in pitch than A, and C is higher in pitch than B, then C is higher in pitch than A. It is clear then that every sound (and we distinguish sounds from noises by just this criterion that they have clearly perceptible pitch) lies in this single linear series of pitches, each at its own fixed point. The order is one-dimensional, to use a convenient term, and it is also not cyclical. And no sound can be removed from this given pitch order. Nor can anything enter this order except sounds. By virtue of being what we call a single sound, a note has to be at a particular pitch; and to be at a particular pitch is to be at a point fixed in the single series of all the pitches that there are.

The important fact for æsthetics is not merely that a musical sound has its particular place in the single order of all pitches, but that we cannot help hearing it at this place, not too exactly always, but necessarily as relatively high or relatively low, and always as higher or lower than any other note whose pitch we can distinguish from its. The serial order is thus native to sound as such. It is intrinsic to sounds in the sense that every sound is in this serial order and that nothing that is not a sound can possibly be in this order. It is this orderliness, as we have seen, that makes concrete pitch patterns in successive notes a possibility. Sounds differing in pitch always lie near-in-pitch-to, and far-in-pitch-from, other sounds. In any given set of notes we can therefore speak of the pitch distance or interval between them, once we have established a measure for such distances. How measure is established is quite another matter, to be considered later in some detail. For the present we need only emphasize the fact that we have here a basic structural possibility, the necessary condition of melody, for example, in so far as melody is pitch pattern made up of a succession of notes at distinguishable intervals from one another, and heard as at these intervals. And this quite regardless of any special set of intervals chosen, or of our having technical musical names for the intervals.

That this is more significant than the mere fact that sounds vary is plain, if we think of smells or tastes. Loudness and softness in sounds, the dimension called their intensity, may be said to be paralleled by intensity in smells or tastes; but only very roughly even for our perception. And our control over the production of smells for example, for direct patterned presentation, is so far behind our control of sound intensities, as with our own voices or by means of instruments, as to be almost negligible. Of pitch, our control, far from being thus negligible, is both accurate and of the wide range defined by many instruments. And what in smell or taste corresponds to pitch in sound? That aspect of an odor or a taste, no doubt, that is specifically characteristic; what defines it as resinous or fragrant or putrid, or salty or sour. Even so we have rather a complex of dimensions than a relatively simple line of variation, a somewhat confusing or confused quality, more comparable to the complexity of timbre, perhaps, than to pitch. And what could be said to lie exactly, or even very roughly, as far from the odor of pine needles in one direction as some other given odor lies in another? The directions of variation here are not plain to ordinary perception. As our systematic knowledge of smells and tastes grows, we can discern order in them, and even without this they themselves furnish æsthetic content as elements more or less alike, more or less contrasting. But just as there is no clear, complete order in them directly apprehended by us, which is intrinsic to their nature as pitch order is to the nature of sounds, so in composition with them we have no adequate control of structural forms or distinctly perceptible intelligible patterns.

It is plainly enough the felt pitch relations, depending upon the intrinsic order of sounds in pitch, that give to music the possibility of melody, so far, we must repeat, as melody depends on pitch for its heard character. That it does so depend characteristically will hardly be denied. A pattern of noises or of sounds of unvarying pitch, or of sounds not at recognizable intervals in pitch, we do not even call melody; and if we did, it must be granted that this would be a melody lacking the distinctive character that melodies in the more usual application of the word are defined by.

Sounds then do not merely vary; they vary systematically. They vary in the two directions of a serial order, along the line of a single dimension. As we shall later see, this allows us to select a limited number of points on the line at recognized intervals, those relations of pitch distance out of which all of our western musical compositions have been made.

But in this emphasis on pitch, we must not neglect the other dimensions of variation in sound. For these are equally conditions, though less strikingly characteristic conditions, of musical structure. The relation louder-than, with its converse, softer-than, is a relation establishing for all sounds—and for all noises, too, so that noise can enter strictly into structure—another one-dimensional serial order intrinsic to sounds and noises, found, that is, in nothing else and always present when sound or noise is present. It is the fact that noises, even with no distinguishable pitch, have their fixed places in this dimension of loudness-softness that makes them possible as integral elements in genuine musical composition. And here again there is not mere variation or mere contrast or similarity, but distinguishable degrees of similarity and contrast, distances in loudness-softness as measured along a single dimension, at one fixed point of which every noise and every sound lies by virtue of its degree of loudness, where also it is heard to lie, if we hear it at all.

For color variation the serially ordered aspects are not quite so easy to exhibit. But at least we have an adequate scheme of them, in which every aspect of variation appears to be systematically included. While the distances between variations differ according as we use one or another of the various color diagrams—the color cones of psychology or the color body of Ostwald's theoretically more regular and systematically more easily intelligible scheme —still the fact of serial orders or dimensions dictated by the intrinsic nature of color variation remains the same. There are the hues from yellow through orange and red, and on through purple and violet to blue and blue-green and green and green-yellow back to yellow. There are the lighter tints for each hue, running up into white in all of them, and the darker shades running down into black. And there are the variations for hues at all degrees of lightness and darkness from maximum saturation to the neutral grays. This gives us three convenient main dimensions of color variation, all compactly illustrated in the familiar diagram of a double cone. The neutral variations, white to black through the grays, are represented along the vertical axis from upper to lower apex; the saturated hues lie on the circumference of the double base; the pure light variations (which may be thought of as mixtures of pure saturated hues with white) run upward to white itself on the surface of the upper cone; and the pure dark variations (which may be thought of as saturated hues mixed with increasing amounts of black) correspondingly run downward on the outer lower surface to black. The points beneath the surface, inside the cone, would represent all the rest of the possibilities of color variation. In general, the downward direction is from light to dark, the direction inward to the axis is from saturation to neutral, and the variations along the circles with centers on the axis, in planes parallel to the base of the double cone, are variations in hue, at all the various intensities and various saturations. To fix convenient points on the circumference of the base of the cone, the complementaries red and green, and yellow and blue, may be placed at the extremities of diameters of this base circle, the two diameters lying at right angles to each other. Thus the circumference is quartered red to yellow, yellow to green, green to blue, and blue back to red.

The scheme fails to represent accurately some of the relative distances as measured in terms of felt degrees of similarity and contrast. Full saturated yellow is not for our vision so far from white as any of the other full hues; and the hues on the red-yellow sector are brighter and warmer than those on the blue-green sector. Moreover, it is obvious that any line through the cone at any angle will give a set of variations along a dimension that constitutes a series just as clearly as the sets of variations along the traditionally selected three lines. But these three are those that have been conventionally named, and they serve our purposes well enough. For all that we wish to establish is that every color variation is to be found somewhere in the scheme, and that therefore every color variation lies at a determinately felt distance from others along any single dimension chosen.

But it will be clear at once that the selection of scales of color variations is guided by relations peculiar to color and not strictly parallel to the relations that make up musical scales. For in color, although hue is perhaps fundamentally characteristic, variations in hue are no more significant for color composition, no more characteristic of color design, than variations of saturation or of brightness. The order of the hues is cyclical, too, while the orders of the variations in saturation and brightness are not. In sound the two serial orders, that of pitch and that of loudness, are like these latter in being non-cyclical. But while notes are regularly named by their pitch—an indication of the greater significance of pitch than of loudness to musical pattern—colors are named sometimes for their hue, sometimes for their other aspects, or for at least two of their aspects in combination. A name like brown is nowhere applicable on the main lines of variation that we have indicated. Nor is brown a "hue." Its "hue" is orange, and yet the name orange does not fit it at all. In fact, of course, it is a name covering a range in the sector about orange, which depends for its characteristic concrete quality largely on being not a saturated color. The fact that we so often speak of browns and grays together as contrasted with reds and greens and yellows and blues, shows how the feeling of its lack of saturation has been taken as its distinguishing characteristic without reference explicitly to any scheme. But the ordinary scheme definitely includes it, and its name, instead of removing it from the scheme, fairly indicates its place there, provided we attend to its characteristic meaning and not merely to the name itself, which might lead us to think of it as one among the other hues.

But another point occurs at once. A pitch pattern is easily recognizable as an aspect of melodic structure and hence of music. But pictures are not so regularly or so readily apprehended as being color patterns. In fact, in much of what we think of under the term painting, it is spatial design not color design that is the characteristic distinction. The parallel with music is still clear, though obviously not at all adequate. As colors are spread over surfaces, so notes are extended through time, and rhythm may enter into melody as distinctly as pitch itself, though a definite rhythmic beat may be entirely absent, as in plainsong. At any rate, it is perfectly clear that painting has not traditionally been sheer color design to any such degree as that in which musical composition has been pitch pattern; and although temporal spread is as necessary a condition of music as spatial spread is of painting, it seems at least fair to say that the relative emphasis on the intrinsic nature of sound in music as distinguished from its one-dimensional extension in time, is greater than the relative emphasis on color as such as distinguished from spatial design in painting.

In both cases, however, it is clear not only that the qualitative orders require either spatial or temporal extension of their elements in order to be concretely present to an organism, but also that the spatial and temporal aspects of the concrete content are themselves structural.

Like pitch, time, whatever else it may be, is an order. That space is an order we all realize from an elementary acquaintance with geometry. Two lines on a surface can not remain merely separate lines. They are necessarily related as parallel to each other or at an angle, and at a determinate angle. And these intrinsic properties of all spatial elements lend themselves to structure, carry structure in their very nature. But without visually perceptible, that is to say colored, area, no spatial pattern can be sensuously present. Even figures in geometry must be black against white or gray if they are to be seen. So that the qualitative elements of our intrinsic qualitative orders are as necessary to the sensuous presentation of spatial character as spatial character is to the presentation of elements of color, or duration and succession in a time order to the presentation of elements of sound.

Two different orders must combine, so to speak, if we are to have any concrete pattern at all. Philosophically this was recognized by Plato in the notion of the communication of the categories. Since every sound in order to be heard, and every color in order to be seen, must be more than pitch and loudness in the one case, more than hue and saturation and brightness in the other, spatial and temporal structure and the orders intrinsic to space and time are as essential to concrete æsthetic surface as what we usually call sensuous content as *distinguished* from spatiotemporal structure. Since, however, we can conceive color and sound abstractly in qualitative orders neither spatial nor temporal, this distinction between so-called content and formal structure lies within concrete content. In fact the distinction of form from matter or of structure from content is entirely relative. We never have the one without the other in actuality. They are both abstractions. And just as this is nothing derogatory to them, since it is true of all the aspects of concretely experienced data, so it is fairly absurd to speak as if qualitative elements and orders were less fundamentally significant in composition than spatial and temporal elements and forms.

Our vastly greater systematization of what we have distinguished by abstraction of the features of the spatial and temporal aspects of our world in mathematics and science inclines us to neglect the significance, even for the arts, of the serial qualitative orders intrinsic to color and sound. We have used mathematical and geometrical abstractions so much that the elements among which these abstract relations subsist have literally vanished, as points have become by definition the vanishing points of lines, and lines the vanishing points or disappearing boundaries between intersecting planes. Space and time have become purely formal as we have realized their abstractness in systematic analysis. There are no real but only nominal elements of space and time. But it takes very little meditation on the nature of pitch and hue to see that once we abstract their formal nature in the same way from sound and color, these latter become purely formal too. It is the lack of full attention to what we mean by color contrast itself, as distinguished from the spatial presentation of such contrast, that makes us unwilling to admit that color as such has no extension, but is only an abstract formal scheme, just as pitch is a purely formal continuum, which is one of the analytical aspects of sound. And adequate analysis would resolve sound totally into such formal aspects, if we treated sound as we do space, and dropped out of our account of it its feeling in concrete presentation.

Thus our scheme of æsthetic analysis may be accused indifferently of formalizing æsthetics, or of reducing all the formal aspects of art and nature to sensuous content. The point is that any content concretely presented, anything experienced directly, is qualitative; that no concrete quality is absolutely simple, that all the surface of the experienced world as clearly apprehended consists, upon analysis, of elements intrinsically ordered and also ordered spatially and temporally. The temporal cannot be present except as it attaches itself to what is qualitatively and spatially extended any more than the qualitative can be altogether unenduring. What is extended in no way at all is nothing. Our purest spiritual longings are the longings of an organism, and they are inconceivable as concretely existent in separation from it. Only in abstraction are they clearly conceivable and at all intelligible, just as color contrast or pitch pattern is conceivable in abstraction from the concrete. Thinking about things in order to know them involves just such abstracting; and it appears to be our good fortune to live in a time when men have penetrated far enough into the nature of logic to allow analysis to be clearly discerned as constituted of the forms which such abstracting makes out. All science involves the discriminating of elements and relations necessary to generality and systematization. The established sciences are the fields where this process has developed sufficiently to give us confidence in the usefulness and validity of the method.

One further point seems required here if we are to be sure that we have not misplaced our emphasis on qualitative orders. We have spoken of these orders as intrinsic to sound and intrinsic to color. We have spoken of spatial and temporal orders as intrinsic to elements that are spatial and temporal. And we have noticed that for actual concretely apparent surfaces for ear and eye we require spatio-temporal structure as well as qualitative structure. A note must have duration just as truly as it must have pitch or timbre; and spatial and temporal structures can appear only as qualitied. We keep "quality" as a term for the very purpose of distinguishing such aspects of color and sound from extensional aspects whether spatial or temporal.

Why, then, are the qualitative orders any more intrinsic to sound and color than spatial or temporal order? And why, if we are to be rigorous, are temporal and spatial order any more intrinsic to spatial and temporal elements than the qualitative orders, since only as qualitied and hence as involving qualitative orders, can either spatial or temporal elements appear concretely? That the answer is in the end a matter of definition must be plain. But good definitions serve honest purposes, and we do not distinguish and define usefully where there is no significant difference. The difference in our case is, however, easy to indicate. Every sound has a pitch and lies in the pitch order, as every color has brightness and saturation and hue and lies in these orders. Also every sound has temporal duration and every color, spatial extension. But everything in the world has duration, while nothing but sound has pitch, as nothing in the world but sound has loudness in the specific use of the word as here applied. Vast numbers of things in the world have spatial extension, while nothing in the world but color has hue or what is meant by brightness or darkness as these terms apply to color. What we are doing is simply to limit the application of the terms that we use to abstract aspects of experience in a way that appears at once to be unambiguous and to serve the purposes of the sort of knowledge that we seek by indicating relevant distinctions for æsthetics.

No concrete experience is totally æsthetic. No æsthetic experience is totally of color or sound or space or time. No color is totally hue; no sound is totally pitch. But it is hearing sounds as at particular pitches and of particular durations and in particular successions that we call hearing music. And it is only by abstracting from the infinite, unintelligible, impinging world of nature what our attention can take in as something or other which is not everything else, that we have distinct experience at all, what Mr. Dewey calls experiences as distinguished from mere vague awareness or bare experience as continuous. And here he agrees with one of the great modern mathematicians who has said that the fundamental intellectual act is the discriminating of the discrete out of the continuous.

Abstraction is necessary to distinct experience of anything as distinguished from anything else, as distinguished from just everything all at once in one totality of confused awareness. Further abstraction is necessary to experience of any particular sort, nameable as æsthetic or not. Still further abstraction is necessary to discriminating what is seen from what is heard or what is tasted from what is smelled. And still further abstraction is required to realize the elements of structure that constitute satisfying appearances in nature and art. Adequate knowledge of all this must also systematize the abstractions. Ideal æsthetic knowledge, absolutely ready response, would bury the whole system of discriminations in our nerves and our

habits, so that the hearing of even a great new symphony
would be an intelligible experience, where every element
was immediately apprehended in those manifold relations
that constitute the genuine sensuous structure that the
symphony actually is. But if the whole were not consciously *felt*, our perfected æsthetic knowledge would be
knowledge of nothing; it would achieve the ideal of abstract science which is expert operation without æsthetic
content. But so long as we remain human creatures with
conscious awareness, there is no danger of arriving at this
state of transparent perfection. We shall remain instead
at that æsthetic stage of experience which at present defines us as characteristically human, neither dissolving into
the flux of natural process in a perfected adaptation that
removes all individual character nor faced with a totally
chaotic unaccepted mass of external pressure with no intelligible quality.

Thus our analytical base is outlined. The elements in it
are elements of sensuous content intrinsically ordered, elements that are found by means of discrimination in the
concrete, but ordered and conceived in abstract series. The
serial orders are of at least two sorts, qualitative and spatio-
temporal, the former intrinsic to certain qualities, the latter to space-time configurations. And from their intrinsic
orders elements cannot be removed. A note carries with
it its position in the pitch series into any composition, and
maintains its determinate distance in pitch from notes of
other pitch placed near or far from it in any temporal succession of notes. In the same way any configuration in
space or time simply exhibits selected parts out of the
ordered manifolds that constitute the nature of space and
time. And as qualities cannot appear concretely except

within spatio-temporal structure, so spatial and temporal configurations require for concrete exhibition qualitative content. The qualitative orders and the spatio-temporal orders are equally abstract, but they are clearly distinct in nature, and while they are dependent reciprocally for concrete exhibition, they are independently variable.

The possibilities for structure are thus infinite; and the arts have selected out of these infinite possibilities a relatively limited number of determinate modes or fundamental patterns on the basis of which works of art have been constructed. Moreover, artists have had to consider many non-æsthetic aspects of the physical media that are the bearers of æsthetic form and quality. And æsthetics is forced into considering such media, and various non-æsthetic purposes, if for no other reason than to distinguish practical technique and practical knowledge of structural materials from what is strictly æsthetic knowledge of æsthetic structures and their constituents as æsthetic surface. The relatively simple analytical basis just outlined is no doubt fundamental and even necessary to æsthetic comprehension. But we shall have to account on non-æsthetic grounds for a great deal that would otherwise remain inexplicable. Our present need is to exhibit those natural conditions that have set up for us ordered and limited selections of elements and basic patterns for composition with these elements.

CHAPTER III

NATURAL BASIC STRUCTURES: SCALES AND OTHER ABSTRACT PATTERNS

I T WOULD be highly satisfying for theoretical purposes if, having discerned the foundation of æsthetics in serial relations intrinsic to sensory elements, we could build directly on these foundations an equally perspicuous logical structure, progressing from these clearly ordered manifolds, by way of their structural relations, to more and more complex wholes, and arriving finally at a complete description of the æsthetic aspect of nature and of all of the arts. But neither nature nor art appears to have developed thus indifferently. It is not preferences, we may suppose, that guide nature. But human preferences themselves are natural phenomena; and preference for one form rather than another gives us a better paradigm of the determinate developments of art or even of natural beauty than does *a priori* logic. For logic at best discriminates form in what has it and only then goes on to its supposedly pure possibilities. The conditioning accidents that decide which forms of nature and of organic life develop, and which possibilities either never become actual or, once actualized, fail to survive, are problems not of logic as such but of what is much more difficult, *viz.*, science as applicable and verifiable knowledge of the world.

The difficulty involved in understanding our world

even in those aspects of it that are largely determined through the operations of human organisms is very great indeed. For this world was not created, after all, under the guidance of human purposes so as to be transparently intelligible to men. But this great difficulty should not blind us to the satisfaction that our minds demand, and the characteristically human delight that we experience, in discerning so much of this actual and exciting structure as may become intelligible to us. Nor should we be blind to the fact that such achieved intelligibility is the exclusive ideal of our minds as intelligence, various as the modes of intelligent mind may be. For intelligence has one sole aim that defines its nature. That is to say, we require some degree of familiar intimacy with our world; and since we are human beings, it is humanly apprehensible perspectives that we demand in any case that is to be called knowledge. It is all one whether these perspectives are brought to a focus by telescopes and mathematics or by such a familiar center of co-ordinates as that which makes a coherent process of jumping a rope or manipulating a knife and fork.

Whether, in other words, we employ our minds to guide ourselves comfortably along the simplest paths of everyday life, or through the portentous mazes of the history of civilization, or over stellar spaces, or through symbolic systems where we may be dealing with various orders of infinity, we necessarily condense our subject matter into coherent human perspectives by schemes, sometimes called logical, sometimes not named. Some of these have been learned in infancy and are gradually buried from conscious view in our physiological mechanisms and their habits. Sometimes they are forms of response that still demand for successful functioning a high degree of rigorous attention to consciously realized cues, as when a musician reads a difficult new score or a scientist the recordings of his complicated instruments. The active intelligence in such operations is, to a degree that we may easily forget, what Locke called only habitual knowledge. It is not the presence in conscious perception of meaning or content, but such readiness of response as, for example, follows a modulation in music perfectly accurately without explicitly realizing its structure, except as the very effect that the less instructed but attentive ear of an ordinary auditor may take in. Or it is such response as records readings accurately at a rate that leaves no time for seeing them as visually full data, or answers a question without having any full consciousness of what language the question was in, or reads a page and gets exactly its sense without being conscious of the words themselves or the sentences. Finally, what is intelligibly grasped may be totally describable in the articulation of an exhibited formal scheme, all of which lies open to conscious attention, as when the figure in a geometrical demonstration offers to direct spatial intuition one case of the embodied meaning of a theorem.

Knowledge in general is only very slightly made up of fully articulated imaginal content of this sort. But for all that, knowledge is knowledge at all only as it is conscious or unconscious adaptation by way of such coherent schemes as, in the modern sense of the term logic, are to be called logical structure. To say that such schemes are merely abstract and logical is only to repeat that they are intelligible, that they are capable of embracing such determinateness as all actual knowledge must have in its objects to make them into objects for it at all, and not merely felt presences, vague in character and not controllable through action.

What, then, are the conditions that have selected and defined for us intelligibly apprehensible structures in the æsthetic surface of nature and the arts?

Perhaps the simplest illustration is our western musical scale. What has selected the intervals that constitute this scale is the way in which sound is physically produced. Sounds with clear pitch occur when bodies like strings or columns of air vibrate at certain rates. Any physical body has its own particular rate, at which it must be set going if it is to vibrate at all. It insists on this rate, so to speak, and no other. And this is no more of a miracle than that any physical thing has its own particular size and weight and hardness. That is to say, vibratory rate is one aspect of the determinate natures of things—their very essence, if Spinoza was right.

We are all familiar with this fact in the dependable regularity in time of the swing of a pendulum. At a much earlier age than that at which we begin to learn formal physics, we most of us learn this law of the pendulum by our attempts to make a rope-swing stop suddenly or hasten its return swing. The harder we push, the longer is the upward flight, and the return refuses to begin until the fixed temporal period of the swing itself is up. So of those balanced rocks whose huge tonnage the efforts of a man can set going. Such balanced masses of weight are ready to take the slightest occasion for embracing their native rate of oscillation. If we have never run across these phenomena, every one, I suppose, has at least twanged a stretched elastic band or rubbed his finger round the edge of a thin goblet and seen the vibrations ripple the water in it while a clear sound is emitted. When vibration rates are rapid enough and not too rapid a sound is produced with definite pitch. It is these familiar natural facts about the determinately timed vibration rates of physical things, and their correlations with higher and lower pitches in the sounds emitted, that have selected for us out of the continuum of pitch, illustrated, say, in a siren, those particular points that mark the intervals of our scale. These intervals then which constitute the scale have been selected for us by nature.

To follow through and to decide on them all took a long time. The scheme was partly discerned by Pythagoras. It was not fully completed and thoroughly grasped until the seventeenth century; and it remained for Bach at the beginning of the next century to exploit it to the full and thus to standardize the basis of western music for two hundred years or so. This was done long before the work of Helmholtz in the nineteenth century indicated clearly the physical facts involved. But now that we know these facts in clear general outline, it becomes easy to see how, in the selection of the scale notes, human ears were guided by the nature of the physical conditions of sound production. We can see, that is, how nature gave us the notes of our scale by giving us the determinate modes and rates of vibration that produce musical sounds at determinate pitch intervals.

A few further facts are basic. Larger bodies vibrate more slowly than smaller ones, and sounds produced by slower vibrations are at lower pitches than sounds produced by more rapid vibrations. Thus a short stretched string produces a higher sound than a longer stretched string. And obviously any part of a string in vibration would sound a higher pitch than the whole of the same string, simply because the part is smaller than the whole and therefore vibrates more rapidly. But when a string is vibrating as a whole, its parts are in general also vibrating as parts, the halves giving their pitch, the thirds theirs, the quarters theirs, the fifths theirs. So that when a string produces a sound, although a great deal of what we hear is at the pitch corresponding to the vibration rate of the whole string, a large part of it also is at the various pitches corresponding to the vibration rates of the fractions of the string.

The pitch given by the vibration of the string as a whole is called the fundamental, *the* pitch of the sound. Furthermore, rates of vibration vary inversely with the length of the vibrating string. That is to say, the vibrations of the half-lengths are at twice the rate of the whole, those of the thirds at three times this rate, those of the fifths at five times. And the sounds at pitches corresponding to these rates make up so large a fraction of the volume of the sound heard that sometimes the fundamental does not even stand out clearly.

How these facts led to the selection of the intervals of the western scale is still not clear. What they show us at once, however, is that the sound of any note at a given pitch, produced in our ordinary ways, has other pitches in it as a large part of what we hear when we hear it, and that all the constituent sounds, which are called partials, are either at the pitch of the fundamental or at higher pitches. The most prominent of them, that is simply the loudest of them, the one making up most of the sound after the fundamental itself, is what we call the octave, which is produced by the vibration of the half-length of the string. It is easy to see then that the so-called octave, when sounded

without the fundamental, that is to say by setting up vibrations in a separate string, half the length of the original
string, will sound like what we heard before. Naturally so,
since it *was* heard before as a large part of the sound which
we called the sound of the fundamental. It is on account
of this fact, *viz.*, that this so-called partial or overtone is so
large a part of the sound heard as the fundamental, that
we take it as the "same" note "an octave higher" and name
its pitch by the same name, the C an octave above an
original C, or A and the A an octave higher. If these are
taken as notes in our scale, the fundamental as the key-note,
then the fundamental is called the Tonic and the other the
Tonic over again. Thus the whole pitch continuum is
marked off into octave lengths in pitch, and it is within one
octave that we select the notes at those intervals that make
up our scale pattern. The scale will thus be a pattern in
pitch established by pitch intervals. The pattern runs
through one octave and is repeated in every other octave.
Instead of one long line of pitches, we have a single short
sequence of them repeated over and over.

The next loudest partial after the octave is what we call
the fifth of the scale of the fundamental. That is, the hearing of a sound with a determinate pitch includes not only
the hearing of its octave but also the hearing of its fifth.
Both of these are parts of its sound, the octave produced by
the vibrations of its halves (vibrations at twice the rate of
the whole), the fifth produced by vibrations of its thirds
(vibrations at three times the rate of the whole). Of the
pitches defining our scale intervals we have so far then,
besides the octave itself, found only this one, the fifth or
so-called Dominant. The Dominant is at a pitch corresponding to the vibrations of the thirds of the string, or at

a vibration rate three times that corresponding to the pitch of the fundamental. Since dividing the length of the string into halves doubles the vibration rate, and into thirds multiplies the rate by three, instead of speaking of a note with pitch corresponding to the vibration rate of half the string length, we can speak of this same note as at a pitch corresponding to a vibration rate twice that of the rate of the fundamental, and so on for vibrations of a third of the string length, a fourth, a fifth, and the rest. A pitch corresponding to a vibration rate twice that of another pitch is the pitch an octave above this latter. Hence multiplying a vibration rate by two or dividing a rate by two will give the rates of pitches an octave above or an octave below but not any pitch at a shorter pitch-interval from the original note. And it is these intervals between, making up the scale, that we are looking for. The one of them that we have so far found, the Dominant, is thus most closely related to the fundamental or Tonic in the sense that a considerable fraction of the sound heard as the Tonic itself is at this pitch of the Dominant. And this pitch is at a clearly heard pitch-distance from that of the fundamental.

In ordinary strings and in the human voice, this pitch interval, or pitch relation or distance, is given to the ear directly in the sound of the fundamental itself. But if the Dominant is thus related to the Tonic or fundamental, as part of its sound, it is plain that the Tonic is in exactly the same way related in pitch to some note below it of which it is in turn a constituent part. This note is called the Subdominant. The heard relation of the Dominant to the Tonic is the same relation as that of the Tonic to the Subdominant; and these three notes constitute the basis of the scale. To repeat. The Dominant is the most strongly audible of the partials given in sounding any note, except just the octave itself. The Dominant is the pitch corresponding to vibrations of a string as divided into thirds, or, if we choose to put it so, it is the pitch corresponding to a vibration rate three times that for the fundamental. The pitch relation of the Dominant *to* the Tonic is exactly the pitch relation of the Tonic *to* the Subdominant. In terms of direction and pitch distance the Subdominant is as far from the Tonic in one direction as the Dominant is in the other. For those familiar with the terms, what we have now found, if our Tonic is C, is the Dominant G along with the Subdominant F; or the Tonic, Do, the Dominant, Sol, and the Subdominant, Fa.

The next loudest partial after the fifth in the sound of the fundamental is that produced by vibrations of the quarters of the string, vibrations the rate of which is four times that corresponding to the pitch of the fundamental. But as the pitch corresponding to twice the vibration rate of the fundamental is the Tonic itself an octave higher, so the pitch at four times the vibration rate for the fundamental is an octave above that octave, the Tonic over again still higher up in the pitch range. The vibration of the string in fifths of its length producing the next most audible part of the sounding fundamental, is at a rate five times that of the fundamental and gives the note at a pitch correspondingly high, a pitch called the Mediant of the scale, roughly half way from Tonic to Dominant, E if the Tonic is C, the Mi of our Do, Re, Mi, two octaves above. And this Mediant, defining the interval called a third, is, like the Dominant, given to the ear in the production of any single note with a clear fundamental pitch. Thus for any

note that we choose and call our Tonic, we have now found
the notes related to it as its Dominant, its Subdominant,
and its Mediant, and defining the intervals named fifth,
fourth, and third. We have also made out the sense in
which the pitches of these notes are related as at given pitch
distances in the actual sound of the Tonic.

If we now add the fifth, fourth, and third of the Dominant and Subdominant, the pitches at those intervals that
are most audibly defined in the sounds of the Dominant
and the Subdominant themselves, we shall have all the
notes of the scale. These are the notes related in pitch to
the Dominant and Subdominant respectively as the Dominant, the Subdominant and the Mediant are related to the
Tonic.

If the Tonic is C (do), the Dominant is G (sol), the
Subdominant is F (fa), and the Mediant is E (mi). Of G,
the Dominant of our Tonic C, the Dominant is D (re of
our scale), the Subdominant is C (our do over again),
and the Mediant B (the si or ti of our scale). Of F, the
Subdominant of our Tonic C, the Dominant is C, the
Subdominant B-flat, and the Mediant A (the la of our
scale). Thus we have C, with G, F, and E; do, with sol,
fa, and mi. We have G with D, C, and B; sol, with re,
do, and si. And we have F, with C, B-flat, and A; fa, with
do, si-flat, and la. In ascending order this gives us C, D, E,
F, G, A, (B-flat), B, C; do, re, mi, fa, sol, la, (si-flat),
si, do. The B-flat does not belong to our present major scale
but to the minor. We may in this account simply omit it,
as in the history of music it was gradually omitted in favor
of B; though in the time of Queen Elizabeth it was rather
an alternative to B than a rejected note belonging to another mode. The Tonic occurs not only as fundamental

but as Subdominant of the Dominant, and Dominant of the Subdominant. And we should expect this of course, since it was the relation of the Dominant to the Tonic that defined the interval from the Tonic to the Subdominant. The Tonic is thus central. It is the note to which the Octave, the Dominant, the Subdominant, and the Mediant are directly related by the intervals most clearly defined in its own sounding partials, the octave, the fifth and the third. And it is the note to which the rest of the scale notes, re, la, and si, are related through the Dominant and the Subdominant.

Another way in which these intervals may be seen as selected by natural conditions is by calculating *a priori* in terms of vibration rates. Here the results of choosing the "most simply related" notes in terms of multiples of the vibration rate of the fundamental, give us once more just the notes that have been historically chosen (determined, that is, by heard relations in pitch) as those of our scale, both major and minor. And since these simplest multiple rates correspond to those pitches which most audibly define the intervals we can distinguish in the sounding fundamental itself, the fact that this calculation gives us the notes of our scale, as this has actually developed in the history of music without any such calculation, should be thoroughly convincing as to the naturalness of the selection of the intervals, the sense in which nature is responsible for our long and painful choice of a scale pattern.

In making the calculation, we must remember that we are placing the pitches for all the intervals of the scale within one octave. To do this requires multiplication or division of vibration rates by two, to raise or lower a pitch into this single-octave range.

Let us consider the rate of vibration giving the pitch of the fundamental to be x. Thus x vibrations per second gives the pitch of the Tonic. The halves of the string will vibrate at the rate 2x. This rate produces a sound at the pitch called the octave. The rates corresponding to pitches between the fundamental and its octave will run from x to 2x, or, omitting the x instead of repeating it after every number, from 1 to 2. (The actually current rate for "middle C" is close to 260.) A vibration rate of 3 gives a note above the octave, which we may bring down into the octave between the Tonic and the octave above it by dividing by 2. This is the vibration rate $\frac{3}{2}$, the pitch corresponding to which is thus the nearest related pitch to the Tonic itself. It is the Dominant, as above, and we may indicate it from now on as D, the Tonic by T, and the octave of the Tonic, or the Tonic an octave above the fundamental, as O. But if the pitch most nearly related to T is D, with a vibration rate $\frac{3}{2}$ (the note a fifth above T), the pitch to which T is related in the opposite direction just as simply and definitely (in fact by the *same* relation or interval) is that pitch corresponding to the vibration rate $\frac{2}{3}$. Pitch relations have direction as well as distance because, as we saw, the relation defining the serial order of the pitches has a sense, upward or downward. If the vibration rate of D is related to that of T as $\frac{3}{2}$ is related to 1, or as $\frac{3}{2}$x is related to x, then T is related to some note below it as 1 is related to $\frac{2}{3}$. In figures, if $\frac{3}{2} : 1 : : 1 : y$, then y equals $\frac{2}{3}$. Or three halves is to two halves as three thirds is to two thirds. But this rate, since it is less than 1, and since the less the vibration rate the lower the pitch, corresponds to a pitch below that of T. Multiply it by 2 to raise it into our octave, and we have the rate $\frac{4}{3}$,

which lies between 1 and $\frac{3}{2}$. The pitch will therefore lie
between $T(1)$ and $D(\frac{3}{2})$. As a matter of fact it is the
rate corresponding to the pitch of the Subdominant (SD)
which we have now placed in the octave, the bottom of
which is our fundamental. The pitch relation by which D
is related to T is thus the same *interval* as that by which
T is related to SD.

The vibration rate 4x is twice 2x, hence the Tonic over
again. The vibration rate 5x gives us a pitch far above O,
but dividing by 2 twice brings it down to $\frac{5}{4}$, a rate between 1 and $\frac{4}{3}$. This is the rate corresponding to the pitch
of the third or Mediant (M) in the octave with which we
are dealing. Thus we have $T = 1$, $M = \frac{5}{4}$, $SD = \frac{4}{3}$,
$D = \frac{3}{2}$. The vibration rates are in these ratios, and the
pitches correspondingly related to the Dominant and to
the Subdominant will be seen to be as follows, where we
simply multiply the vibration rate of D and SD respectively
by the same fractions we have employed on T. The results may be tabulated as follows: The first table multiplies
the vibration rate of the fundamental or Tonic by $\frac{3}{2}$, by
$\frac{4}{3}$, and by $\frac{5}{4}$, and gives the rates corresponding to the
intervals of the fifth, the fourth, and the major third,
establishing the position of the Dominant, the Subdominant, and the Mediant within the octave.

Table 1

$$T = 1$$
$$1 \times \tfrac{3}{2} = \tfrac{3}{2} = D$$
$$1 \times \tfrac{4}{3} = \tfrac{4}{3} = SD$$
$$1 \times \tfrac{5}{4} = \tfrac{5}{4} = M$$

As in this table we have derived the D, the SD, and the M of T, so in the next table we may derive the D, the SD, and the M of the Dominant.

Table 2

$$D = \tfrac{3}{2}$$
$$\tfrac{3}{2} \times \tfrac{3}{2} = \quad \tfrac{9}{4} = \text{ D of D}$$
$$\tfrac{3}{2} \times \tfrac{4}{3} = \quad 2 = \text{SD of D}$$
$$\tfrac{3}{2} \times \tfrac{5}{4} = \tfrac{15}{8} = \text{ M of D}$$

Lowering the Dominant of the Dominant into the octave between 1 and 2, gives the rate $\tfrac{9}{8}$, which is the second degree of the scale on the fundamental. The Subdominant of the Dominant is the Tonic an octave higher than the fundamental, and the Median of the Dominant is the seventh degree of the scale on the fundamental. In the same way we may derive the D, the SD, and the M of the SD, as follows:

Table 3

$$SD = \tfrac{4}{3}$$
$$\tfrac{4}{3} \times \tfrac{3}{2} = \quad 2 = \text{ D of SD}$$
$$\tfrac{4}{3} \times \tfrac{4}{3} = \tfrac{16}{9} = \text{SD of SD}$$
$$\tfrac{4}{3} \times \tfrac{5}{4} = \tfrac{5}{3} = \text{ M of SD}$$

These are the octave once more, the flatted seventh degree of the scale on the fundamental, and the sixth degree of the scale. Thus the ratios that we find are, in the order of their magnitude:

1	$\tfrac{9}{8}$	$\tfrac{5}{4}$	$\tfrac{4}{3}$	$\tfrac{3}{2}$	$\tfrac{5}{3}$	$(\tfrac{16}{9})$	$\tfrac{15}{8}$	2
I	II	III	IV	V	VI	(VII-flat)	VII	VIII

With the exception of $^{16}/_9$, these are the actual ratios of the vibration rates of the pitches marking the intervals of our scale. If 1 is do, $^9/_8$ is re, $^5/_4$ mi, and so through the eight degrees. And the $^{16}/_9$ was for a long time, as we noted above, an equally acceptable alternative to $^{15}/_8$, which establishes the interval of the major seventh.

In other words the intervals making up our scale are not simply arbitrary divisions of the octave, but intervals given by the pitch relations defined to the ear within any single sound which has clearly distinguishable pitch. Notes at these intervals have these determinate pitch relations to one another, and the intervals are thus dictated by the heard constituents of any actually sounding note. The constituents are heard at definite pitch intervals from the fundamental; and it is these intervals that were first learned and finally grouped in the scale as we now have it; or rather as it served western music from the early eighteenth century to the late nineteenth. The selection then was the discerning of those intervals that any sound as physically produced most emphatically defines. It is not that the notes of the major scale are all sounded in the sound of any given note, but that the intervals, the pitch relations, the determinate distances in pitch called fifths, fourths and so on, are defined in the partials, which lie at these distances from the fundamental or from one another. In hearing any note sounded, then, we have heard the interval called a fifth, the interval called a fourth (for the fifth is a fourth below the octave of the fundamental, which is one of the most prominent of the partials), and the interval called the third. And this by hearing only the first five partials, which are clearly apparent.

That there are other partials defining other intervals,

that intervals may be differently related and grouped, that smaller or larger intervals exclusively would serve the purposes of melody and hence of harmony (any two notes at a given melodic interval necessarily define that interval harmonically as well)—all these are obvious facts. The purpose of the present exposition is only to point out how one particular set of intervals, chosen historically, is based on definite physical conditions, those involved by nature in the actual production of any musical sound by means of a vibrating body. The relative prominence of the partials in the human voice is very much the same as in a string—involves this same series of overtones that defines the intervals of our scale—and western music has used voices and strings most characteristically. It is strings that vibrate in pianos, as it was strings that vibrated in harps and clavichords and harpsichords. And while the more prominent partials of brasses and woodwinds do not in their order of loudness follow the simple rule that the octave, the fifth, and then the third, are the most clearly heard partials in this order of prominence, the one fact that this order is commonest in voices and strings, is enough to indicate the naturalness of the basis defined.

If the sense in which nature is responsible for our selection of the intervals that constitute our scale structure is clear, we must not forget, however, that this set of intervals is an abstraction. We have been finding the natural conditions that select sounds at certain pitch intervals, because pitches defining these intervals, or distances apart in pitch, and making up the sound of any one note called the fundamental only in reference to these other pitches in it, sound loudly enough to be distinguished by the ear. But what we have in the scale itself is a set of pitches; not sounds, but points in the pitch continuum; not concrete notes, but the distances that mark off our intervals. The timbre of the fundamental (which is the effect of all the partials in it combined in a distinctive quality); the loudness necessary to our hearing either the fundamental or its partials, and to discriminating the intervals so defined; the duration required for hearing any note at all at any pitch or of any quality or loudness—all these are essential to concrete musical sound and to discovering the scale. But they are all left out in the scale structure itself. For this is a scheme within pitch alone, pitch considered as distinct from timbre or loudness or duration, pitch as points along the serial order of pitch itself, and limited to those selected to make out the scale. Pitch without these other aspects of sound cannot be concretely heard, but is an abstraction derived from what is heard. And we hardly need to remind ourselves again that it is this abstraction that is the basis of conscious musical composition as well as of its apprehensible form in the classic centuries of our western music.

Here then is a structural form discerned in nature as an aspect of sounds physically produced, a scheme of intervals defined for us in the very nature of musical sound, but abstracted from this concrete objective presence to sense in a scheme of abstract relations or pitch intervals. This is a scheme not discernible anywhere but in sound itself. It is discerned by means of discriminating human ears as an intelligible form just because we see it as a set of relations making up a pattern or structure. What it establishes is a set of positions in pitch, dividing the pitch continuum into octave-length units, and dividing the octave-length into steps of determinate magnitude in determinate order. It was only after these steps were chosen and fixed in this succession that the terms octave, fifth, and the rest, to name the eight places of the scale-order, became applicable.

Thus it is a series of abstract elements that we have found as the scale, along an abstract continuum of one dimension. And of course these elements remain also in the order intrinsic to that continuum itself, and thus constitute a very limited series selected from, and lying within, another series. Every note in a piece of music written in a key—and keys are simply the scale as beginning on any particular note—lies in its particular position either above or below any other note in the key, and related now not merely in this above-below order but at a definite scale interval or distance, a second or third or fourth or fifth or sixth or seventh or octave, or the sum of two or more of these, a ninth, a tenth, and so on, above or below any other note in the music. The intervals given us to discriminate in the production of a sound constitute these pitch measures, or measures of pitch distance. And notes sounded at these distances from one another in pitch give the concrete specific effect of the particular interval. A fifth has its distinctive character or quality, as have all the other intervals. Moreover, on account of the way in which all the notes of the scale are related to a basic pitch, the fundamental, and through this to one another, there are now resting points, especially the Tonic and the Dominant and Subdominant, and points that demand further progress, and progress in a given direction. The Dominant is not so final as the Tonic, nor so urgent in requiring us to move to another pitch as is the second, for example; and the seventh calls so definitely for the Tonic that it requires no formal musical training at all to feel this demand.

This is the same sort of intelligibility that we have in geometrical patterns, where, from the apex of a triangle, say, the lines run *down* to what we call the base, and require our eye to follow them all the way without stopping, as we could very well do in a pattern like a hexagon. All the parts of a triangle are related to one another in ways that we understand so soon as we grasp the figure geometrically at all, see it, that is, as a triangle. The sum of the interior angles will be a straight angle in the same way as that in which the sum of an interval and its inversion (the complement which added to it fills out an octave) will make up that pitch distance of which it is felt to form a fraction. As an angle of thirty degrees plus one of sixty degrees make a right angle, so a major second plus a fourth make a fifth. As two right angles make a straight angle, so a perfect fourth plus a perfect fifth makes an octave. Not that there is any complete parallel, but that there is in one case as in the other a set of abstract elements in clearly perceived relations, so that the structure itself is felt to be intelligible in being constituted of these relations. As the façade of a building may be, from the point of view of spatial design, a rectangle with a triangular space over it, with other rectangles for doors and windows, and with triangles of specific shape, or curves of determinate curvature, over these; so a piece of music is made up, from the point of view of pitch, of seconds and thirds and fourths and fifths and sixths and sevenths, all in relations which are finally analysable into the fundamental scale intervals that we have made out. Melody and harmony simply deploy pitch elements in accordance with the possibilities offered by the selection of elements and relations that make up the scale. What at first seemed merely the natural physical process of sound production is thus manifested as the defining basis of a set of elements in intelligible qualitative order—an order, that is, within pitch as such—that is as clear a structural basis as geometry.

The fundamental pitch continuum is one necessary condition of this basic scale structure; the nature of the production of a musical sound, with its partials, is another. And it is this natural selection out of an ordered continuum that offers those infinite structural possibilities that have been exploited historically as classical western music.

Music depends on many other things, of course, and our classical western music is only one among a great number of musical possibilities. The point here is simply that any structure, any work of art that is consciously composed and that is intelligibly apprehensible, is so only by virtue of such basic structural character, depending, in the case of sound, on a native qualitative order in elements and a naturally guided selection of these in an abstract system of relations.

Such natural patterns of intrinsically ordered qualitative elements are the basis of any art. The scale thus illustrates several general principles in æsthetics. First, that specific qualitative orders like those of pitch and hue are necessary conditions of composition in certain media. Second, that out of the infinite possibilities in any such qualitative manifold, some natural mode of selection of elements is required to make up a firm basic structure out of which the more complex concrete structures of art are developed. Third, that this natural pattern is abstract, and hence that whole movements in the developments of the arts consist in the exploitation of such naturally selected but abstract patterns.

As the western scale is only one among many standard

interval patterns in pitch, so pitch patterns are only one among many varieties of standard patterns in the arts. In color, for example, scales have been selected out of the intrinsic color orders, and variations memorized as at definite color intervals from one another, in specified color dimensions. But while the facts of harmony and contrast, and hence of all color design as such, depend absolutely on the intrinsic qualitative relations of color variations, color intervals have not been (and apparently cannot be) discovered on any such basis as would give us exactly five or seven or ten points along a dimension. Even the hues number three or four or seven or twelve or twenty-four, depending on what scheme we adopt. In music we sometimes use the pitch continuum itself, as in sliding along a violin string or singing *portamento* instead of proceeding always by the use of notes at definite intervals from one another. But these are only special incidental musical effects. Such directional movement without definitely fixed and clearly felt intervals is much more characteristic in the spreading of color over an area than in the spreading of sounds through time. And although there is an enormous number of possibilities for color contrasts of different degrees and along different dimensions, the lack of any universally accepted scale of color intervals suggests the reason why color design as a strict parallel to pitch pattern does not constitute one of the arts, however great the rôle that color plays in painting or in such minor arts as pure geometrical design in glass and in fabrics. That there is color structure as such follows from the fact that there are orders native to color variations, as sketched in the preceding chapter. And much of the confusion in discussing color in painting is due to our common knowledge of this order only in its extremes, black-white, red-green, *etc.*, and its directions, full saturation to neutral gray, red to orange to yellow, and so on; and not in clearly defined scales along clearly distinguished dimensions of variation. We all recognize variation from lighter to darker, and we all recognize the emphatic contrast produced by juxtaposing colors that lie far apart in hue or in one of the other color dimensions. But these are comparatively gross and unmeasured distinctions, especially as named in our far from systematic or complete color terms.

So-called scaled palettes have been worked out with great definiteness and are fundamentally useful for teaching. Attention to one such scheme over a period of diligent practice results in an ability to distinguish the particular selected color variations much as many ears distinguish pitches—sometimes so exactly that the term *absolute pitch* is used as if it named a peculiar faculty instead of merely a high degree of discrimination in aural memory. For many of us it is correspondingly accurate visual memory for color that allows us to dispense with most of such explicit systematic knowledge of color variations, and relations among colors, as would correspond to a grasp of intervals and key relations in music, without missing the actual color effects that interest us. And it is also true that sometimes feeling for pitch intervals in their structural relations is rather less marked in those gifted with so-called absolute pitch, than in those not so gifted.

It is plain enough, however, that apprehending a painting—much more so with works of sculpture and architecture where color is likely to be less important to design— has as much to do with spatial forms and relations as with grasping intrinsic color relations in definite color intervals.

And most of the great painters of history did not have strictly scaled palettes, but rather such points fixed in color and color combinations as available pigments furnished, and as the colors given in nature upon objects—sky, leaves, flowers, flesh, jewels, fabrics—led them to recognize and to desire. It is equally plain that a great deal of painting sought, even in color itself, not merely naturally suggested single colors, but also such color contrasts and harmonies as various natural appearances in the world suggested and made familiar to men and acceptable—the yellow of gold or the brilliance of jewels against flesh or colored fabrics, the blue of sky and distant hills against the dark green of cypresses or the gray green of olive trees, the bright hues of flowers on the varying greens of foliage. Color combination as such, directly composed out of the systematic possibilities, occurs much more emphatically in modern painting than in the classic masters. And even here, since color is spread upon surfaces, the patterns of painting are never bare color design and seldom *mainly* color design. Even so-called abstractions are at least as fully the deploying of geometrical forms and relations, as of the notes in a color-scale, or even of any less definitely measured color variations.

All of the arts are composite, of course. A pitch pattern requires time for its concrete presentation, and qualitative orders themselves, whether scales or not, require spatial or temporal orders for concrete exhibition. The relative degree to which one kind of order rather than another constitutes the concrete structure of a work of art is not a very significant question for æsthetics or for artists, so long as we discriminate the elements and the orders that do actually function in the apprehended structural whole.

We have been putting such emphasis upon qualitative order mainly because theorists of all sorts, æstheticians as well as teachers of the arts, have so neglected both the absolutely essential rôle played by such orders in making up the characteristic quality of particular sorts of composition in any art, and the specific structure of these orders themselves.

With this once emphatically stated, then, and examples given first of the intrinsically qualitative orders, and then of one selected qualitative pattern, *viz.,* the musical scale, it is safe enough to go on to basic patterns in the more regularly recognized kinds of intelligible form. For general æsthetic theory we must limit ourselves here. We cannot in any brief account, even if—impossibly—we were acquainted with all the works of all the arts, trace the innumerable cases of development of naturally given or suggested basic patterns, either out of the fundamental intrinsic orders themselves—qualitative, temporal, and spatial —or into their countless concrete developments, by way of selection, combination, and the intentions of genius, where not only intrinsic qualitative and temporal and spatial orders may all be combined, but also the basic patterns themselves, and in infinitely complex modifications.

But an adequate æsthetics would carry out an account of just such developments; and for any intelligent understanding of the nature of art we should have clearly in mind the nature of such patterns in general and examples of their varieties in different fields and in different degrees of complexity, hence at different levels of intelligibility.

The account given above of the scale is only the barest beginning of a realization of the possibilities of even this scale itself, not to mention the system of keys, all related

by means of aspects of its structure and the modifications
of it called the minor modes. There are also all the earlier
scales, the Greek modes and the ecclesiastical modes, and
any number of other scales with intervals of different
lengths and arrangements of these in different sequences.
We have not gone far enough here even to make fully apparent the actual nature of the steps and half-steps that are
our own smallest intervals in classical western music. But
all of this could be done on the basis outlined above, by
following a good elementary account of the physical
foundations of music and the elements of harmony. What
we should now notice is that not only pitch patterns but
some pattern in time—with duration and succession of
sounds—is essential to the simplest of familiar melodies,
and that the time patterns of music are all built up on
basic temporal patterns of the very simplest sorts, familiar
in breathing and walking, in the fact of two sides of our
body, and in the *three*'s presented by any central feature
with the two others at the right and left of it, the nose
between the eyes, the tongue between the two lips, a valley
between two ranges of hills, a river between two banks.
Embodiments of twoness and threeness in our experience
of nature, and of natural motions, are of the commonest
occurrence and extremely easy to discern. Combinations of
two's and *three*'s, and multiples of these, give us almost
the whole foundation of the purely temporal aspects of
musical form, as well as of verse rhythm. But the basic
abstract patterns of verse rhythm require a more adequate
account. For the present we shall be content to indicate
some of the fundamental naturally defined patterns that
have formed the basis of some of the spatial arts.

There is no more striking example of a particular elementary spatial design from a natural source that has functioned variously in the plastic arts than the form of the acanthus leaf. For centuries, in wood, in metal and in stone, this particular pattern, very much simplified after all, as a glance at a growing acanthus plant is enough to remind us, furnished a decorative element adapted in itself to easy apprehension, but also to combination, not only by repetition in varying positions but with other functional shapes of all sorts, the curved bodies of vases, the pedestals of fountains, the capitals of columns. So definitely did it become formalized, that its resemblance to the growing leaf is often no greater than to scores of other leaf forms. In the course of its various adaptations this conventionalization of it as a formal element was carried so far as to be felt as an essential part of the definition of one of the orders in architecture. Its familiar occurrence in classic ornament sanctioned it to later taste and made it not only acceptable, but, like the too convenient formulas of language, often not genuinely expressive. From being a graceful and effective convention for design, it often degenerated into being *merely* conventional, a tag instead of a vital element.

It is at this point in the development of sensuous forms, as in linguistic idioms, that easy familiarity turns into transparent intelligibility, æsthetic content thus disappearing. What is gained in facility of understanding by the extreme degree of familiarity of such words as our articles and conjunctions, for example, is lost in emphatic force or accurate determinacy. In scientific language, where the medium functions ideally to the degree to which it disappears as medium, and presents its meanings directly by virtue of both paucity and definiteness or even uniqueness of learned denotation, this tendency serves the central purpose of the discourse. For art it is the negation of the function of the medium of presentation, which itself constitutes the æsthetic content. So far as structural elements in the arts arrive at the degree of familiarity that turns them into bare cues to structure, and allow us thus with a minimum of consciousness to grasp what is before us, so far we lose the æsthetic character of that which, before it became so familiar, took our attention in a response the object of which was clearly realized and emotionally felt æsthetic surface, a fully present consummation.

The simple geometrical forms that men earlier in history sometimes took to be the most beautiful of all objects, are illustrations both of this gradually lost æsthetic content and of the essential need of the very transparency which, unless it is integral to further content, is æsthetically nothing at all. The pure intelligibility of geometrical forms, like the circle or the triangle, or the rectangle in the proportions of the golden section, seemed to Plato the mark of æsthetic purity and perfection. And even nowadays critics sometimes point to the triangularity of a religious painting not merely as its general form, but as if somehow this form were a signal virtue. There are two equally important points here to notice: the absolute need for intelligible form, and the vital need for having a form not already totally familiar. Without apprehensible form no composition coheres sufficiently to be one presented objective for attention; on the other hand the most familiar of the geometrical figures by themselves have little expressive vitality.

The variation within the field of even the most familiar polygons of geometry—kinds and degrees of symmetry and other orderly aspects—has been fully made out in

Mr. Birkhoff's chapter on polygons in his *Æsthetic Measure*. But whatever his formula may measure, it is not degrees of beauty, since if the degree of beauty varies directly with the orderliness of the figure, and inversely with its complexity, a maximum would be reached when the "order" became infinite or perfect, and the complexity vanished. But, as we have seen, this would be to reduce the structural form itself to the perfectly transparent, to that which we grasp without conscious attention and so without appreciable æsthetic content. Or, to put it a little differently, the absolutely orderly on this scheme would be the perfectly simple; but the perfectly simple by definition lacks all complexity even of form, and all sensuous content. Even a square has four angles, four square corners, four equal sides, and so on, and it stands in one position or another. It has also an enclosed area and some color.

To be a structure of any sort means to be made up thus of discriminable elements in relations. When there are no elements to be discriminated as related in a complex, there is no complex present, no structural whole and hence no æsthetic surface at all. But Mr. Birkhoff's analysis of polygons should not, in fairness, be considered at this mere abstract level. It is enormously valuable in pointing out, on a clear basis of defined spatial relations and spatial elements and character exclusively, how loose and confused and misrepresentative are such terms as *balance* and *symmetry* as so generally employed by æstheticians and critics. Mr. Birkhoff is a courageous pioneer, who makes it plain that even in this one field of a limited number of fairly familiar plane polygons—a few of the most elementary two-dimensional spatial structures as such—symmetry stands for half a dozen different actually appreciated aspects of spatial organization. And this is to say nothing at all, of course, about the many other aspects of spatial structure, nor about the scores of analogical and thoroughly muddled applications of the terms *balance* and *symmetry* and *rhythm* to temporal and qualitative structures and relations, and to combinations of all these, with many further complexities, that supposedly serious critics and theorists apply as "principles" to thousands of kinds, as well as to particular works, of the arts.

An æsthetics which is based on the sorts of orders and of elements that we have made out, and which takes into account the obvious fact of the adoption of ready-made natural selections of elements and relations in basic patterns, also finds a place for the useful in art and in æsthetics. It is not merely that use is an aim in many of the arts that construct æsthetically satisfying objects, but that uses define objects and hence their forms. And these useful forms, like naturally suggested forms, are immediately intelligible *as forms,* once we have become familiar with them in their uses. An ordinary spoon goes far beyond the geometry at the disposal of most of us. From the *a priori* geometrical standpoint it is a highly complex and difficult configuration. But its use has sanctified its shape to us, and, as always, the familiar becomes the intelligible. So of knives and forks and chairs and tables and musical instruments. So of houses and windows and roofs and triangular gables, and of the proportions of supporting columns that would be absurdly unacceptable as isolated rectangles in some other position or function.

And so of course of animal bodies. These shapes have reached a complexity scarcely imaginable to men were they not so familiarly presented to us in our world that we have learned them. And so particularly of the human body. Artists, fascinated by this shape for a thousand reasons, began by copying some of its most obvious outlines. In Egypt the human body was taken as a strictly canonical pattern from which no divergence was allowed, once the formulated proportions had been chosen. Even in Greece it took centuries to arrive at the free use of the shape of the body for the expressive purposes of art. And the Egyptians never gave up their adherence to a strict canon. If in the long history of their sculpture some tendency towards a fresh naturalism in details marks what seem to us some of their most directly stirring achievements, the characteristic defining modifications in the styles of the various periods appear to be clearly related to measurable differences formulated in the canonical set of proportions itself, not the free use of the pattern as a merely underlying norm to be modified at will by the artist.

When we admire the few relatively freer works of Egyptian art or the flowering of Greek sculpture, we should remember both the natural origin and the abstract formal nature of the canon itself. For it is only as variations on some such extremely well-defined norm that a sculptured body has any determinate characteristics at all. Long arms are long only in relation to the body; but they are long also in proportion to *any* body only by virtue of the relation of the length of human arms in general to the height of human beings in general, within the proportions, that is, of a defined norm. The proportions in the Greek canon were not those of the Egyptian canon. Polyclitus, whose lance-bearer was *called* the Canon, apparently chose a definite and rather special Greek type; and certainly no Greek body, exactly measured, constituted this norm. For all of us a familiar pattern of the body grows up in our minds and imaginations; and it is only in relation to this pattern that there could possibly be any definite meaning in any descriptive term that would express what we see when we look at a statue or a living body. A torso is flattened here or rounded there only as we have in mind a degree of flatness or a degree of roundness in comparison to which the presented case is flatter or rounder. And such norms are not born in us but given to us by nature through our abstracting processes. There comes to be for each of us a set of proportions among elements oriented in three dimensions, that we apply on any given occasion; and this is obviously an abstract pattern, not a full concrete image with hair of specific color and texture and all the other particularized features, with their vast number of completely determinate peculiarities. It is only the spatial aspect, and the spatial aspect not of one body, but abstracted from many bodies seen. It is a formulated pattern by virtue of which any human body is apprehended as a familiar—that is, intelligible—spatial form, and any work of sculpture as having its own degrees of modification. The norm is thus turned to its proper function, such modification constituting the expressiveness of the work of sculpture, its defining purpose as art.

The two points mentioned above may now be clearer. First, then, these fundamental norms or patterns are essential to any determinateness of form at all, even as bare shape in spatial composition; hence to the apprehension of any determinate form. The intention that is artistic—and apprehension must follow this if it is to be relevant—is not to achieve the standard pattern or to reduce all forms to the simplest possible for beauty's sake. But some standard pattern is necessary in order for us to see what is there at all, though it is not enough to make us see it fully for what it is. The function of the standard is to serve as the sole basis on which determinate character can be either intended or concretely presented and apprehended. For the little boy of a generation ago, whose grandmother's figure from the waist down was a cone truncated at the waist-line and flaring to the ground in two slightly convex curves, the female figures of French painting seemed oddly deformed. And we may possibly hope for some fresh vitality in the appreciation of sculpture, as we already have it in much of the present creative activity of sculptors, from a general public addicted to athletic meets and bathing beaches and beauty contests, though the long and rigorous attention to the human body cultivated in a life-class is no more than adequate to any very fine perception of the body's contours and proportions.

Apprehensibility *alone* is the useful—not æsthetic—aim of the employment of media of communication, when what is to be communicated lies not within the medium itself as deployed to sense, but beyond it by way of conventional reference. Learning consists largely in absorbing the forms of things as symbols of other things, so completely as to be able to respond habitually and unconsciously to the medium in view of what it leads to in action or theory or what as symbolism it denotes. But while æsthetic objects, in order to be such, must employ basic intelligible norms or patterns to be determinately apprehended at all, the understanding of these patterns, the completely familiar grasping of them, which acquaintance with nature and human products as well as the cultivation of the arts brings about, would be theoretical grasp, recognition of technical elements, formal principles and abstract patterns, not æsthetic experience but at the best æsthetic theory. Our second point, then, has been that such normal established patterns never constitute the concrete individuality of the form of any work of art.

Æsthetic experience is its own present end and aim; and we shall see later that taking it as merely theoretical or technical knowledge is studying it as if its function were that of language in science, where language presents to us through a medium, as nearly transparent as possible, what we are actually interested in and what is not directly present. The æsthetic is what is present in the medium apprehended, and all that needs to be transparent is so much of the constituent structural relations and elements as will put us in a position to grasp the functioning of these. This functioning is the presentation to us of the individualized content, which is not exhausted in merely recognized familiar forms but is the objectively embodied æsthetic expression itself.

CHAPTER IV

TEMPORAL PATTERNS: VERSE RHYTHM

THE test of any scheme of analysis comes with its application to actual forms of art in actual artistic works. That would be reason enough for spending the effort here to discriminate some of the basic temporal patterns that are integral to verse structure and that constitute at least one specifically distinguishable aspect of what is loosely called verse rhythm. But in the scheme that we have been expounding there is, besides this reason, the need for some exhibition of temporal order and temporal patterns on their own account. For what we have so far made out with any degree of fullness is only one of the qualitative orders, that of pitch, which is peculiar to sound as independent of time, and secondly that particular basic abstraction totally within the pitch order that constitutes the pattern of our musical scale. Spatial order and basic spatial patterns have been pretty fully recognized and used in analysis, though their fundamental nature has never been specifically worked out, so far as I know, with any degree of adequacy to their various detail or to the definite distinctness in their varieties of spatial character, except in the limited list of plane polygons of Mr. Birkhoff's *Æsthetic Measure*. Even there the analysis is treated somewhat incidentally as in the main a means to measuring æsthetic value; and this by way of a formula that appears more and more dubious the more strictly it is taken as an evaluating measure, that is, the more strictly it is taken as performing its purported function in Mr. Birkhoff's æsthetic theory. But the Birkhoff analysis of polygons and the examples of basic spatial patterns suggested in the preceding chapter sufficiently illustrate the fundamental nature and importance of the spatial patterns that function so widely in the arts.

The one sort of pattern that we have not yet even so much as explicitly illustrated is the sort that is constituted abstractly out of the time-order, an order clearly distinguishable from what we have called qualitative orders, as in sound and color, and from spatial order, as in all space forms. For these two reasons then, *viz.*, the filling out of our scheme of analysis by an account of temporal order and pattern, and the application to a medium in one of the arts of this sort of basic pattern, we may well turn to the temporal order itself and then to some of the basic temporal patterns exhibited by English verse form. A third end may also be served by the present chapter. It will suggest the answer to the most pointed objection to our whole scheme.

This objection is simply that we are working backward into the obvious aspects of æsthetic structure and attending to what is of no use or interest, instead of working forward from the accepted basis in established conventions and media to complexities and characteristics that need explication. This is only one form of the objection to philosophical analysis in general, which makes an attempt to get to fundamentals, no matter how simple or obvious, in the hope that subjects apparently thoroughly confused and difficult may appear simpler and clearer on a better theoretical basis.

This objection has been most emphatically raised and most elaborately exploited in the case of the logic of verbal discourse. No one denies the validity of Aristotelian syllogism; but most of us are only too likely to feel that this is so abstract and so simple a doctrine that in applying it to reasoned discourse we falsify the structure of the discourse by the simplification. When once our abstract falsification is clearly stated, we have to offer as analysis nothing beyond two principles that every one assumes without question and has no need to study. These are (1) that *is* and *is not* are incompatible in a single simple assertion in meaningful speech and (2) that *some* and *all* are to be clearly distinguished from each other, especially in drawing inferences. But it was not by denying but by correcting the doctrine of syllogism, and then by developing an account of the type of relational structure so discerned, that the fuller range and the specific actual function of logical analysis were discovered, and the syllogism seen in its strictly logical form and in its proper if minor place in systematic logic. If, even after the lapse of all these centuries with their results in learning, we could do anywhere nearly so well with æsthetics as Aristotle did with linguistic logic, it goes without saying that we should be more than creditably occupied in this twentieth century. At any rate the present attempt is both called for in our scheme and clearly relevant in its application to verse structure. And it is to be judged, as is also the scheme of which it is a systematic part, only on the basis of its service to intelligibility in the arts, in the case at hand the intelligibility of the temporal aspect of verse rhythm, which in turn is one aspect of verse structure.

That verse *has* a temporal aspect need hardly be argued. And that this temporal aspect is intrinsically ordered is equally obvious. The nature of that order is, however, not so plain. But whatever time may mean, one temporal characteristic is the irreversible one-dimensional order in which any and every given sequence of events occurs. And, since the syllables of verse are sounding events that come one after another in time, they are obviously in an order of temporal succession. But this is not their only temporal aspect. In reading verse we do not fill all of the time that elapses with the sounds of syllables. There are pauses of various durations between and even within words, and the syllables themselves vary in the time that their sounds occupy, so that the temporal pattern is not exclusively that of the number of syllables in groups. What the syllables do temporarily, as they sound successively, is to indicate a pattern in time which their own sounds partly fill. And to discern the purely temporal aspect of the pattern so constituted, we shall have to notice the elementary nature of the temporal order itself and the kind of pattern that is possible to elements in such an order just because of their occurring temporally.

Temporal elements are for actual apprehension durations of whatever endures, periods of time marked by what fills them. And we must remember that in being periods of time they are not spatial lengths. Their sort of length is a longer or shorter duration, not a spatial distance. The danger is that language may confuse us on the point. For we use *length* to refer to space as well as time, just as we may use length to refer to the sizes of pitch intervals,

But time involves motion, and hence rapidity or rate of motion; time is apprehended only in change and usually thought of as a flowing on of events. While it is thus clear that every temporal pattern must have some specific rate, however variable, it is not this rate, not the fastness or slowness, that is the chief characteristic of the temporal patterns of verse. In music, rate is very important indeed. It is the whole difference, for example, between a slow hymn tune and the same tune as a lively dance. The tune, that is to say, varies very markedly in character with its rate, even if we keep the same pattern of pitches and of relative durations of notes and rests. Verse also varies in rate; but only within the relatively narrow conventional limits of intelligible speech. For verse is after all only a mode of intelligible speech. And while definite changes in tempo change the whole feeling of a piece of music and the effective character of its rhythm, the slighter changes possible within the ordinary limits of rapidity in speech, while they are obviously significant to its general effect, are not ordinarily felt to be what chiefly characterizes its rhythmical form or even its strictly temporal pattern. We might indeed speak of the same rhythm at a slightly different rate without offending the most sensitive prosodist.

But if rate is not a primary consideration in the temporal aspect of verse structure, what characteristics of a temporal order are left to give it structure at all?

As we have already seen, time order is one-dimensional and irreversible. And if a movement in one direction and in one dimension, the rate of which does not greatly vary as affecting structure throughout the whole range of speech, is to constitute a pattern, then we must find the elements of this pattern by marking divisions along this one dimension. There seems to be no other possibility, so long as it is strictly temporal structure that we are considering. In other words, since it is not the absolute lengths of time involved, their length, that is, in terms of the units of time of our established clocks, it must be their relative lengths, the temporal relations of these lengths to one another. But we can apprehend no particular lengths at all without some indication of them. We can have no definitely related lengths of duration, or to speak more cautiously and correctly, no temporal relations of durations to one another, unless we have a unit duration. And since all that we directly apprehend in verse is sound, it will have to be some aspect of sound that marks off clearly related time-lengths or durations along the one dimension of time itself and thus defines a unit of time.

But in order to mark off a time-length, a duration, both ends of this interval must be indicated. This is what brings into any temporal pattern in verse a recurrent interval of time, a unit of temporal length, or as it is usually called, the *measure*. In music the term *measure* has taken on so close an association with the section of a staff between two bar-lines that we almost forget its actually fundamental function of measuring off time even in musical rhythm itself. In verse, the term *measure* has lost force and precision by loose usage until its meaning has become extremely vague. The old terms, *measure* and *number,* however, as applied to verse, if only we notice their actual primary meanings, indicate the two aspects of verse that give it strictly temporal structure.

First, however, to notice recurrence a little more carefully. Verbal explanation will not make the fact of recurrence clear unless we are willing to pay attention to the

familiar data of simple direct experience that we are talking
about. Experiment is demanded, though only of that easy
sort that we can readily carry out in imagination. To mark
the two ends of an interval of duration, it is necessary to
give two signs, one at the beginning and one at the end.
But doing this (by whatever method, say merely pronouncing *one — one*) if no further indication is given,
will inevitably be taken by our attention as indicating not
merely the interval between the two sounds, but also a
second interval, following the second pronouncing of *one*.
And this second interval will be felt as of the same length
as the interval following the first *one* and terminated by
the second *one*. With the tapping of a pencil, or with a
repeated gesture, or two flashes of light, the same result
follows, provided only that the interval between the two
signs is short enough to be grasped in the span of direct
attention as a single duration. For of course time runs
on continuously, and there is always a supply of it to fill
out a second duration immediately following a marked
one. To some ears a duration of equal length is also defined preceding the first *one,* as soon as the second *one* has
indicated this length between the two *one*'s; so that we
have at least two and perhaps three intervals of time
marked by the two signs necessary to mark the beginning
and the end of one single interval. The pattern is laid
upon the continuum and felt as patterning it all, until
some further sign comes to mark a new and different
division, or until attention flags or is distracted by other
content.

Temporal patterns using a measure longer than the
span of direct æsthetic attention may be recorded as *rep-
resenting* a temporal pattern in some graphic medium, or

they may in various ways be imaged representatively in memory or abstractly conceived. But for direct apprehension neither season after season, nor day after day, nor death after life, is a literally felt recurrence of temporal interval, not a direct æsthetic datum. Such so-called rhythms may be *represented* æsthetically or recognized conceptually; but they are not in their own temporal duration and character presented in experience. They are represented by something *else,* which is directly experienced. They may be symbolized, not given. This is due to a limitation of our modes of apprehension. Time intervals have to be relatively short to be directly felt as definite durations, recognizable, rememberable, felt temporal lengths. For any temporal pattern at all, then, we require a relatively short measure, indicated to attention at both ends, and so involving its own recurrence. So much for the basic fact of a fundamental measure in any sort of temporal pattern. What now of the other aspect of this pattern indicated by the word number, the "numbers" in which Pope lisped because they came?

Once given a measure it is clear enough that we have a simple pattern in the recurrence of this measure. Instead of continuously flowing time, we have time punctuated and divided by the beginnings of measures. Or to put it from the other point of view, we have time built up as the sum of a number of equal successive durations. That is to say, we have a sequence of constituent simple parts, all alike, making up a temporal whole by following one after another along a single dimension. The resemblance of this pattern to that made by the division of the pitch continuum into successive octaves is obvious. A great difference between the two, however, lies in the fact that we seem to have no particular length of time, dictated by the nature of events merely in virtue of their temporality, to give us one unit measure (like the octave in pitch) rather than another. Nor have we apparently any further specified divisions of a measure, or groupings of measures, dictated by nature. In this our time scale is more like color scales, where direction is clear but units of distance along dimensions somewhat arbitrary. The pitch continuum was one aspect of sound itself, and the physical production of a single sound indicated to us pitch distances, those between its partials all sounding together, which we discerned as naturally defined and naturally related musical intervals. But everything of every sort that occurs at all occurs in time, and in some particular temporal succession.

We have seen that temporal occurrences that are patterned—as in the swinging pendulum with its regularly timed motion—define an indefinitely large number of rates. If gross natural oscillations are the prototypes of our temporal patterns, then within the limits of our span of attention one measure would appear to be as natural as another and one mode of division or grouping as natural as any other.

The temporal arts, especially music and dancing, illustrate this variety clearly. A slow dance is in just as well defined a measure as a quick one, and in just as clear a pattern. Only the limits of fineness in our nervous muscular adjustments prevent much greater speed, and only the limits of our span of attention much slower speed, from being presented as clearly patterned for direct sensuous apprehension. Within these limits, however, one measure and one pattern is as good as another. From what we have already said, it is plain that this does however involve *some* definitely felt measure, and that this measure recurs. Thus some particular selected measure is essential, though within the limits indicated, no one measure is more naturally suggested to us than any one of many others. And with any one chosen we get successive equal durations marked by some particular sort of sensory indication to attention. The recurrent indicator or beat marks off the recurrent interval along the single dimension of time and allows us to grasp time as divided into a number of intervals of time, time as a built-up structural form out of elements of time related to one another both in succession and in length, numbered and measured. In this simplest case the elements are related as equal in length and neither divided further within nor held together in further groupings; the measure is a fixed duration, and the number is unity. The pattern is then *one, one, one, one,* and so on without variation.

But a characteristic that accompanies this strictly temporal pattern as actually presented will at once be evident. If there are measures of duration marked off from one another at the end points, then our attention will be concentrated on distinguishing these end points, or rather on what indicates them. There will be tension and relaxation, the tension up to the point, the relaxation as this point is announced to sense, and the renewal of attention at once, gradually increasing until it is relieved again by the next point of division, which we are expectantly listening or looking for to mark the end of a duration already defined in our minds, or at any rate in our nervous mechanism of response. While this recurrent tension and relaxation will be merely incidental to our apprehension of the purely temporal aspect of the pattern, it will be very emphatically characteristic of our concrete experience of that pattern. For of necessity the grasp of the pattern varies in definiteness and adequacy with the degree of attention to the precise falling of the point of division on the single line of temporal forward progress. Since our attentive processes will thus be alternately tensed in expectation and relaxed at the points of division, to the degree that we are absorbed by the temporal pattern, a rhythmical structure will be more strikingly and obviously characterized by rise and fall, by ictus, beat, pulse, than by the strictly temporal character of the pattern, which is simply the division of the time stream into measures. Any amateur performance of music or dancing is likely to be an illustration of this, in its overemphasis on the points of division because of a conscious endeavor to exhibit fully the felt structure. What is primary to rhythmical pattern, however, from the point of view of temporal structure, remains the time division into measures. Even if this were not so, what we are here concerned with is the *temporal* aspect of verse pattern, whether or not it is properly to be called the rhythm of verse.

Distinguishing this one aspect of verse form clearly will at least remind us of the complexity of verse structure even when it is considered only in that aspect of it that is found in sound alone.

Having noted the characteristic pulse which constitutes so much of our experience of rhythm, we may now turn to filling out our account of the temporal pattern itself in abstraction from other factors of the concrete experience. The possibilities beyond the simple recurrence of a single undivided measure are obviously the dividing of this measure and the grouping of several measures. The still different possibility of a succession of measures of different lengths is hardly another distinct kind of variation, but only a different grouping of units. For either the measure remains of the same length and is only differently divided, or else the continuity of the pattern—the necessary condition of there being a pattern at all—depends upon taking a subdivision of the "measure" as the recurrent unit that is necessary to coherence. This is illustrated very commonly in modern music, where, say, different numbers of quarter notes, two, three, four, or five, the quarters all having the same even time throughout, constitute consecutive "measures." It is plain here that the conventional meaning of the term measure, viz., what lies between two bar-lines, has become its sole denotation, whereas what does the actual measuring of the elements of the time pattern, is the duration of a quarter note.

The means of indicating all of the further complexities in the temporal pattern of a sound-medium are plainly enough variations in sound itself, louder or softer sound, variations in pitch or other quality, cessation of sound. But since short silences do not in their own nature attract attention, but serve rather to emphasize the sound immediately following, the main indication of all divisions of the flow of a sounding medium in time will be greater sound intensity at the points of division. Changes in pitch may also serve this purpose. But in English in general pitch plays a not very explicit and distinctly minor rôle; even in verse it is not the most natural means of indicating the divisions that mark out the temporal pattern. Concrete poetry as actually pronounced uses a great many means to its ends, combined in an enormous variety of subtle ways. But we shall do little towards understanding this full structure until we distinguish some of its simpler formal aspects with clarity and some degree of accuracy.

Louder sound is not only the simplest way of drawing attention to a given point of division in the flow of verse, but it is one obvious feature of that accent on particular syllables that is so characteristic of spoken English. To be sure, accent does not fall in English words in ordinary discourse at intervals that mark a simple enough time pattern to be apprehended readily as clearly specified. In music, where also slightly increased loudness is the normal means of indicating the beginnings of measures, any element *may* take on increased loudness without changing the pitch sequence, and hence any pitch element may begin a measure; but this is not true in a sequence of syllables in the words of intelligible sentences. If in speech we arbitrarily increased loudness at, say, every third syllable of a sentence, in order to give it pattern in time, we should simply make it unintelligible. Linguistic conventions demand that in *polygamy*, for example, the second syllable and no other take the heavy accent. *Polly-gamigh* is no further from being intelligible written English than the sound of *polygamy* is from being spoken English if we throw heavy accents on the first and last syllables, instead of on the second, where the accent has been placed by custom, following a number of conventions in pronunciation.

The fact remains, however, that accented syllables do give us the chief means of marking off divisions in the temporal stream of English verse. Accent is after all the main factor used for indicating measures. This is the most obviously definite sense in which it is proper to say that English verse rhythm is accentual, unless the term *accent* be used very broadly to mean the ictus in the tension-relaxation experience, which, as we have seen, is highly characteristic and perhaps predominant in concrete verse presentation and its apprehension. Monosyllables are accented or not, but again in accordance with the exigencies of significance; though either relatively heavy or relatively light accent is often possible on the same monosyllable in the same context without offensive distortion of linguistic convention and without danger to sense. Accent, then, is the chief means of indicating temporal measure in English verse as well as the subdivision and the grouping of measures. It is the means used, that is, to mark off into measured and thus temporally related intervals what would otherwise be either an unpatterned flow of words, or a pattern such as we have in prose, a pattern so subtle and so complex that no critical analysis has so far succeeded in making it out at all explicitly or adequately. This remains a pattern, therefore, that is not simple enough to be readily and fully grasped as the clearly temporal form of a rhythm or of a kind of rhythm.

After all this we may say, I think, that we have taken account of the essential function of a fundamental recurrent measure in any temporal pattern, and hence in the temporal aspect of verse structure, and that we have distinguished accent as the chief means in English verse for indicating measure, the subdivision of measures, and any grouping of them into larger temporal units.

Our next question is as to what in nature gives us not merely measures of certain lengths, but acceptable patterns of the subdivision of measures and of their grouping. And it is clear that this is to ask what numbers our verse for us in those ways that have become established in use.

The answer is simply those easiest, because most familiar, numbers of all, one, two, and three. Natural rhythms are likely to be a division into two, forward and back, up and down, right and left, of the patterned swaying of the body, or the waving of the arms, or of walking, or swinging an object, or rocking a crib. The very ticking of the clock we apprehend most easily as *one-two, one-two,* putting in this simple pattern apparently because it gives the ticking a form or structure that we take as sufficient to characterize it comfortably, to turn it into one simple repeated pattern instead of a mere endless and formless string of ticks. But it is perfectly easy to hear a clock tick *one-two-three, one-two-three,* instead of *one-two, one-two,* and to group the *two*'s or the *three*'s into two or three *two*'s or two or three *three*'s. And it is not very difficult to group them into one *two* followed by a *three,* and so on. Almost all of our temporal patterns in music, in dancing, or in verse, follow this general tendency to gather elements that occur regularly in time into groups of *two*'s and *three*'s, and to compound these into larger groupings. What is essential is some regular time division into an apprehensible simple pattern; and it makes little difference whether the main unit is taken as subdivided into smaller units, or whether the smallest units are taken as fundamental, and all longer units as groups of them.

In musical notation, where the indicated divisions of time are relative (a half-note half the time of a whole-note, a quarter-note half of a half-note, and so on), a quick measure is often indicated by writing a time signature as so many sixteenth-notes, or so many eighth-notes, to the measure, instead of so many halves or wholes; but the same composition could of course be written with a different time signature and correspondingly quarter-notes for eighths, or half-notes for eighths. The notation is a matter of convenience as well as a matter of many conventions. And not all of the conventions, though they may be musically significant in various traditional ways, indicate clearly anything about the general nature of temporal pattern in music, except that there must be fixed lengths of duration for the notes relatively to one another, and a measure with a pattern of subdivision. Some particular measure must be indicated and some subdivision of it, not merely by the notation but to the ear.

But we have already seen that the particular rate of the measures of verse, the particular duration of its fundamental measure—since verse is one form of speech—is not of primary structural importance to its temporal pattern. While there has to be such a fixed measure, which is necessarily a specific duration, it is the main subdivision, along with the further subdivisions of this in various ways, that is most characteristic. We do speak of a slow or a quick rhythm; but we speak much oftener, and perhaps more naturally, of a three-rhythm, or a two-rhythm, meaning by the *three* or the *two* the number of main subdivisions of the measure itself, the length of which (a duration) characterizes the rhythm as swift or slow. In verse at any rate swiftness and slowness are not the chief structural considerations. Thus some defined measure along with some pattern of subdivision gives us the whole character of the verse pattern as temporal.

The varieties of form possible in such patterns are very great in number. And the specific means in various media for indicating the points of division that mark off the pattern to attention are also extremely various. Any means of calling attention sharply to a point in time, as experience moves in time's single direction at its inevitable rate, will do—distinct gestures or quick sounds, or changes in sound, pitch change or distinctly greater loudness, anything that can occur sharply enough at a moment to mark that moment for our attention as the end of one interval of time, and the beginning of the· next. Our whole lives are lived in moving process, and process in its bare temporal continuity is unbearably vague and unintelligible—indefinite, formless and meaningless. If we are not to be driven insane by it, we must give it temporal pattern by dividing it into repeatable units; endow it with structural form apprehended as such, measure it and count it.

There is no other way in which we can accept it familiarly and feel at home in it, understand it, control it, and rely on it. For the totally non-structural is the totally formless, unacceptable to apprehension, inconceivable, not merely unreliable, but unthinkable. The temporal aspect of our world, on the contrary, is one of its most elementary formal characteristics, susceptible by its very nature of exhibiting connection, pattern, and meaning in history, in daily life, in all occurrences, and hence in the occurrent sounds of music and verse.

In fact time itself is not a thing, but a word, a general label under which we hold together all these specific temporal relations. Time is not a receptacle in which things endure, but the definite nature of their enduring in measured and numbered ways. Time is the general term for the patterned measure of specifically changing and moving things, from which we abstract the formal temporal character to which we are likely to attribute a being of its own, independent of all that could possibly have this character. Abstracting is so natural and simple and necessary a process for thought, that thinking about the temporal aspect of changing things has led men from early times to speak as if this abstracted character of events were a real something in which they had their being, whereas all the being that time as such has is the abstract temporal aspect of actually changing qualitative content, from which it is distinguished as temporal order. Obviously it is no more independent of changing and moving things than pitch is independent of sounds; and obviously it is no less independent. That is, the temporal pattern of changing things can be clearly abstracted and thought of without thinking of all the other aspects of things, exactly as pitch can be thought of without thinking of temporal sequence, or duration, or loudness or timbre. But this temporal aspect is to be discriminated in all experience, whereas in pitch we have what is to be discriminated only in sound.

At this point the objection that we are to meet in the present chapter becomes most plausible. Granted all that has just been said about temporal pattern; how far does such an abstract simplified scheme help to make clear the nature of verse structure? What have such measure and number as this to do with the pulsing movement of dancing and music, or the subtle and complex rhythms of verse? Our answer will be even plausible only so far as an application of this elementary abstract analytical scheme to actual verse appears to help us discern its heard pattern in so far as that pattern is temporal. And since the scheme has little relation to iambs and trochees and dactyls, or to tetrameters and pentameters, we shall do best to take first some ordinary English words, then some sequences of words, and then some familiar English verse, and apply our scheme directly. But we can do this more intelligently if we keep in mind the resemblance of verse to music in this same respect of temporal pattern.

The musical quality of verse is a loose phrase for many aspects of verse which in some cases have the same nature and in some cases a very different nature from aspects of music proper. For example, music and verse both use pitch variation. But in traditional western music, pitch is regularly a matter not only of distinct measured intervals but of the relations of intervals to one another in a system centering on a key-note. It is a pattern of pitch which can be discovered as independent of rhythm or even of duration or of strictly temporal pattern. In verse, however, pitch is used neither in measured pitch intervals nor in relations of intervals to one another in a system. Pitch of course helps to constitute so-called accent both in music and in verse. But high and low pitch in speech lie in a narrower range than in music, the instruments of music going far beyond human voices; in speech the mere being distinguishably higher or lower is enough. Strict intervals of accurately measured pitch-length simply are not in use, though of course any particular pitch change in the voice that is reading verse *could* be measured and recorded in the terms of the accepted musical intervals, and even of these as more finely made out by physical laboratory devices. The point is that the thirds and fourths and fifths and so on that the ear recognizes as defined intervals in music, are neither consciously used in verse, nor intrinsic, as such specified heard intervals, to its apprehended structure. Rise and fall in pitch is enough, with perhaps some rather vague differences in the amount of rise and fall.

It is also true that even the temporal patterns of speech are less strictly measured and less explicitly felt as specific temporal lengths temporally related, than the rigorously measured temporal patterns of musical composition. But there can hardly be any question as to there being a clearly felt temporal pattern in verse in just the sense in which there is not a measured pitch pattern. If so, there must be measure and number in verse, since without these there could be no clearly apprehended temporal pattern at all. Rhyme, assonance, alliteration, various other sorts of more or less complex kinds of agreement and repetition among speech sounds, characterized by vowel quality as well as by the types of noises in consonants, are undoubtedly musical in the loose sense of the term as applied to verse. But the strictly defined formal characteristic common to the two arts is plainly enough what we call rhythmical structure.

We have seen that temporal pattern is definitely not the whole of rhythm in any of its manifestations. The very character of expectancy involving tension and relaxation, with ictus or accent, takes on its felt character, however, only as it indicates or characterizes this formal temporal pattern as filled out by sound or movement. What we may learn by keeping the rhythmical form of music in mind is, among other things, that the essentials of measure and number, mechanically simple as they are, and occurring as they do explicitly in the sound as well as in the notation, no more constitute full rhythmical structure in music than they do in verse. Hence to make them out clearly in verse is no more to deny the rest of its rhythmical and other structural characteristics than putting bar-lines along a staff is to deny musical phrasing, for example, without which a clearly measured beat becomes altogether uninteresting and unmusical. But as bar-lines and time signatures help enormously to indicate at least one aspect of musical rhythm clearly, so the making out of the strictly temporal aspect of verse as measured and numbered should be a clarification of at least part of what is called verse rhythm.

Those who speak of a rhythm of sense as well as a rhythm of sound merely confuse issues by confusing terms and their meanings. Rhythm is not divorced from sense; but if it is to be apprehended through sound, then we should show how sense makes sounds vary, or how the varying of sound modifies the sense. There is one structure with many aspects, and it is no help towards full appreciation of this structure to refuse to give specific names to one aspect of it at a time. In any verse rhythm, whether conditioned by sense or conditioning sense, some temporal pattern is involved in the sound, or else no such pattern is æsthetically discernible at all as an aspect of its rhythmical character. If we are clear that in considering abstract temporal pattern as such, we are making no pretense to giving an adequate account of the whole nature of concrete rhythms, we need hardly fear the sort of criticism that keeps harping on the fact that such analysis is incomplete. In this sense human thinking is incomplete in being thinking at all; its proper completion is either stopping with the particular results of a particular analysis, before going on to another, or the losing of itself altogether in feeling. In æsthetics the common demand for completeness is the demand for æsthetic experience itself instead of æsthetic theory.

Adequacy in analysis, as distinguished from comple-

ness in the sense of an impossible and meaningless omniscience, depends on clear and definite accounts of distinguishable aspects, integral to co .crete structure. It is
only clouded or precluded by the repeated naming in many
large terms of the felt total character of such structure. In
fact, as with so much literary criticism, the literary accounts of verse form are most of them intent on indicating
by their very use of terms an effect comparable to the
effect of the actual verse itself, instead of analysing or in
any sense explaining that effect in terms of such of its
constituents as can be discerned, and as they actually go
to make it up. And the literary criticism of analysis in
general is like the silly condemnations of psychology on
the ground that psychology does not explain man; by
which is meant, I suppose, that in psychological analysis
one does not find actual human beings parading before
one, but some account of some of the more easily discerned and systematically ordered aspects of man as a
being that thinks and behaves.

There is no explanation in the sense of saying why
things exist in the concrete. There is only the concrete itself, there before us. Knowledge consists in analysing it
with relevance to some point of view and for some purpose.
Complete explanation, in the sense in which it is apparently demanded by those who have not stopped to
think what knowledge necessarily is, would be exactly
that formless uncreated void which is the sole alternative
to a world with specific aspects to characterize it. The
void is itself the obvious explanation of the actual world,
the source material out of which God made it, as we
should all know by this time. If we are not trying to solve
the problem of creation, if we are willing to admit that

there is a world at all, with whatever character it has; then for explanation all that we can look to is analysis, the discerning of the aspects of the world from various human points of view, so that living may be intelligent and not totally the nightmare that men's conflicting interests make of so much of it. We can not prevent sound theory from abetting specific purposes; but we do not need, in the name of completeness of explanation, to take all order and value out of theory itself, and turn even the purported struggle for knowledge into a competitive acclamation of chaos.

Sometimes, in the more rigorous and less literary accounts of verse, one obviously partial aspect of its structure is held up to ridicule because it is not the character of the whole. Or the terms in which this aspect is described are disparagingly contrasted with the connotation of some other term or set of terms, which may either clearly indicate another genuine aspect of rhythmical form, or may simply suggest, by way of larger and vaguer feeling content, a character more plausibly applicable to the whole concrete character of verse itself. In fact the attempt is all too often to be descriptive in terms suggesting an effect like that of verse, terms with large significance and broad emotional connotation, than to distinguish on any unequivocal basis any of the numerous analytical factors involved. And philosophers, who should know what knowledge is, and what analysis can accomplish, fall only too easily into this sort of pseudo-poetic vein and talk of ultimates and absolutes and degrees of reality, as if any one could possibly deal with anything *un*real. What is unmitigatedly unreal is nothing, and the term is meaningless, except as contrasting one kind of thing with another, images with physical things, dream content with the content of waking life, the coherent and the significant with the incoherent and the insignificant. The last distinctions we have are still distinctions of kind or quality; one distinguished from another, not all of them distinguished from what is nothing. For *nothing*, without restriction, means the absence of anything of any kind, and this is entirely unthinkable. *Nothing*, as significantly used in speech, means the absence of the expected content, or the absence of one sort of thing, and this is never anything at all beyond the present feeling that comes of the fact that this thing has left us or has not been attained. We need literary descriptions of all sorts; but for knowledge descriptions are more useful when their terms are unambiguous and systematically connected.

When the description of verse is given in musical terms, it is only too likely to employ these terms in no clearly defined musical sense. It thus gains specious adequacy, apparent sophistication, and rich suggestiveness at the expense of any very clear meaning.

The main obstacle, no doubt, in the way of our understanding verse structure, is the sort of scheme that makes all syllables into units of equal time value and omits all the pauses that would correspond to the rests in music. It then goes on to confound accent with length, so that a syllable may be called indifferently heavy, long, or accented. This blurs the actual function of accent for indicating time divisions, and at the same time neglects those measured durations without which no temporal rhythm is possible. When such a scheme as this is put into terms suitable only to a language which in comparison with English is non-accentual, and in which syllables were in all probability held out like musical notes to fill measures of time, irrelevance is added to confusion. The very units called feet are in English very seldom integral divisions of the measures; and the further grouping into lines of so many feet is not a grouping of measures. The counted number of feet as constituted solely of syllables, instead of being made up in part of time unfilled by any sound, is so completely artificial a description of measured lines that verse like ballad metre, for example, is described as if in time and in rhythm the alternate lines were of different temporal length. And the smooth, familiar, three-measure line of blank verse is described as pentameter, suggesting that there is a division into five, a grouping that would be completely foreign to any traditional, natural time-pattern.

This is the sort of misrepresentation of verse form that has resulted so largely in the dropping of so-called scansion from serious literary study. Even to a beginner it becomes clear that the relation of the scheme to actual poetic form, and to rhythm in particular, is strained and artificial. And prosodists usually do not speak as if, except in the most general way, their account of verse had anything to do with the specific expressiveness of poetry. In fact the usual procedure is to dispose of the form as if it were not expressive but had a character distinct and even separate from the intention expressed in the words, instead of being the aspect of poetic discourse that is most distinctively the expressive power of verse as distinguished from prose. If our present scheme fails to exhibit this structural form fully as it functions, at least what we here offer as analysis is both unequivocal in its terms and directly discernible in familiar verse. Its full functioning in literary expression is not so much the concern of general æsthetics as of the literary study of poetry. But it is hard to believe that any adequate account of verse form will be built up by either misapplied classical terms or loose musical analogies. What seems to be required is an attempt first to discern the temporal pattern itself and the constituents of verse form as temporally integrated, and only then to consider other aspects of the form of verse, all of which together will be required to understand the nature of concrete rhythmical structure, the rich, subtle, patterned flow of English poetry.

Our own present attempt will be limited to discriminating the temporal pattern in two familiar verse forms, iambic pentameter and ballad metre. But we have a difficulty to overcome at the very beginning which is almost impossible to dispose of by mere written discussion. We should have actually to recite the verse aloud, that is, if we are to show that we are not palpably and absurdly misreading it when we apply our scheme. Even the available experimental data of psychological studies would tend to establish our scheme only so far as the reading of verse in such experiments is governed by a clear sense of rhythm. So far as the recording is relevant to the actual temporal pattern on which the reading is based, it would of course take into account the silences elapsing between sound durations as well as the sound durations themselves.

The moments of division of the pattern into measures are often not clearly marked by the beginnings of words or of syllables. In fact, to say when a word or a syllable begins or ends with reference to a time pattern, is not always a matter of recording sounds at all, but rather of distinguishing the nodal point in the rising and falling curve of intensity of attention. To take the parallel of musical conducting, it is obvious that the sharp, clear indication of the beat is a difficult technical achievement. Even for those who are to follow it, it is not a matter merely of seeing gestures, but of grasping a temporal scheme first and then feeling the increase and decrease of intensity in gestures so sensitively that the exact point of division is discriminated, the moment that ends one cycle or measure of systole-diastole and begins the next. The further subdivision must often be carried out in accordance with the rhythmical sense of the player himself, following the musical notation, which indicates this point, with the added check furnished by a necessarily intermittent attention to the conductor's movements. At any rate one would most adequately describe the measure and number of the musical rhythm, what corresponds to the basic temporal pattern of verse with which we are concerned, in terms of the time signature, the indication of the tempo, the traditional interpretation, or the felt embodiment of this pattern in the music. In verse, where we have only tradition to guide us, and no notation to mark the measure or number, we cannot discover the intended or felt temporal pattern *of the verse* even by recording instruments, unless we can interpret the data of a thoroughly trained reader in terms of a numbered and measured scheme which is the very pattern we are looking for, and sensitive modifications of which give the verse its expressive individual character.

This is not to say that experiments do not accurately record facts about particular readings, but that sometimes the facts chosen to record are not strictly relevant to the abstract temporal pattern in the first place, in the ways suggested above. And primarily it is because æsthetic temporal structure is necessarily a directly apprehended pattern, however mechanically inexact, or else not an aspect of verse or of music at all. This is no disparagement of psychological studies of rhythm; it is only noticing that what we are here concerned with is simpler and more fundamental than the subject matter of such experiments. It is rather the definition of what such experiments take for granted. Not that it is not empirically experienced or without its obvious source in nature. Indeed, as we have noticed, its basic character is defined to us in natural movements and in habits of hearing. It is from such movements and habits that we draw—abstract, if we are to keep to the formal term—the character of what we construct and what we apprehend in the specific modifications of such patterns in the arts. The scheme in its ordered elements is given to us to discern and to adopt and elaborate upon.

If one asks what are correct readings, and who is to decide this question, what readings properly exemplify temporal patterns in verse, readings the record of which might be sound data for exhibiting this pattern unequivocally in conventional time units properly numbered, the answer is of course that one does one's best to read rhythmically and then notices the pattern. This requires not only training in reading verse, but in holding consciously to a steady, accurate beat, so that the measure of it is apparent at the same time as the sound of the verse. The beat must be so definitely held to as to constitute a genuinely independent measure, but a measure directly experienced æsthetically. We need the kind of training that music students sometimes get in beating time accurately to their own performances, or in measuring the rhythmical pattern of heard music by means of conventional patterns in gesture. And few of us have such training. Without it we let our beat follow our own irregularities of sound production, or we let it follow not the temporal pattern of music heard but its more prominent aspects in pitch and loudness, thus missing its basic temporal structure altogether. Such a beating of time as is required does not, however, go below the threshold of felt æsthetic consciousness; and the use of mechanical instruments that measure much finer divisions of time than we are capable of experiencing directly may give confusing results, unless the records made by means of them are carefully interpreted. Just as a variation in vibration rate of a fraction of a vibration per second is in general not a difference in pitch for ears, and so not a difference in æsthetic structure in pitch, so measures of irregularity in time pattern in units of small fractions of a second may occur as the record of a perfectly regular time measure in æsthetic perception. Laboratory psychologists of course know all this; but the interpreters of their data often make such use of the records as actually contradicts the relevant findings. The only possible test of the æsthetic structure of pitch pattern, as of rhythmical pattern, is the trained human faculties of direct perception; and if the ear hears a regularly measured flow of verse, then æsthetically the flow of verse is regular and measured. What we are seeking in verse structure is what an ordinarily perceptive ear distinguishes without difficulty in music adequately performed.

Thus, even though we go wrong in details, our general scheme of analysis need not fail to give us the actual temporal pattern of verse rhythm, once we have learned to beat time accurately and independently, and to recognize underlying regular temporal pattern.

To begin a little indirectly, let us notice first not lines

of finished verse, but some obvious differences in the temporal duration of syllables in English words, and some of the more obvious requirements made by conventional English accent on particular syllables. The word *sessions*, for example, requires an accent on the first syllable; it also requires more time for the second syllable than for the first. This would be true in the singular; in the plural it is still plainer. It seems fairly accurate to say that normal English pronunciation fits the word into three counts, one for the first syllable, two for the second. Not that *sions* is necessarily held out quite so long as this, but that one does not start another word following *sessions*, until three equal counts have been filled out, each of the length of time taken for the first syllable. It will be found that this measure of three short counts is customary in a great deal of English speech. To discern this grouping into three counts a sure sense of regularity in a rapid count of three is required; and the reason for our not being explicitly and formally familiar with its characteristic occurrence in our speech is largely that we do not beat time habitually, and that when for some special purpose we do, this group of three counts is likely to be taken all together as the smallest single unit that we explicitly observe.

In *Eat your cake and have it too,* there are two counts for *eat,* one for *your,* two for *cake,* one for *and,* one for *have* and two for *it.* For the final *too,* and because it is in this end position, there are three counts. That is to say, the syllables as naturally spoken fall into this count, the time pattern being felt as *one-two-three, one-two-three,* not as *one-two, one-two.* To pronounce the words in an evenly measured *one-two, one-two* is perfectly possible. It is clear, however, that the temporal division into *one-*

two, one-two would produce an unnatural and noticeably mechanical reading. We may add another few words and get: *Eat your cake and have it too, say I; that's really beating fate and living high.* This can be turned into a so-called pentameter couplet by spacing:

> Eat your cake and have it too, say I;
> That's really beating fate and living high.

To describe this as two lines of five feet each is to disregard the clearly natural temporal measure and grouping. If our count was correctly given above, the grouping in measures is as follows: (Adding the *so* at the beginning does not change the time-lengths of the syllables, and it is now put in to make the couplet match more exactly some of the famous lines of actual English poetry.)

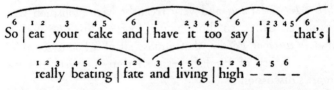

and the couplet does not differ in temporal measure and number from:

> How rash, how swift to plunge himself in ill,
> Proud of his power, and boundless in his will.

To make the two match still more closely, we may invert *that's really* to *really that's.* Then the accents fall almost exactly into the same pattern. There is an enormous amount of English verse not only in Dryden, but in Shakespeare and Milton and Pope, to mention only some of the greatest names, that falls exactly into this temporal pattern.

Almost regularly at the end of the line as printed there is a pause of three beats or so, half of one of the compound measures, filled out by silence, measured, however, just as the sounding parts of the lines are measured. In music there would be rests in the notation to make this clear. As the diagram indicates, the phrasing regularly crosses the bar-lines which mark the measures of the temporal pattern. The comparison with any piece of music, beginning on any but the first note of a measure, will illustrate the way in which musical phrasing also crosses the bar-lines not exceptionally but as often as not. And the reading of any of the Shakespeare sonnets will clearly exhibit three heavy accents to a line, marking three measures. Except for the subdivision of the halves of the measures into three instead of two counts, this is the measure of iambic pentametre given by Coventry Patmore in his essay, *English Metrical Law;* and very recently Mr. Housman has reminded us, in an illuminating footnote in *The Name and Nature of Poetry,* that almost all of what is sensible in the theory of English verse rhythm is given in Patmore's discussion.

Since Patmore's day there have been some stupidly blind criticisms of him; but the general scheme as given in *English Metrical Law* is at least reasonably familiar. What enlightened modern prosodists—though not many of the writers of the convenient hand-books on metrics are among these—have neglected, is the characteristic triple division at the bottom of the scheme, which Patmore also failed to discern. But what is much more important, they seem never to have realized that concrete rhythmical form is complex not merely in the sense of being subtly irregular—as all form is in actual art—but in being constituted neither by accent alone, nor by temporal pattern alone, nor by ictus or pulse, but by all these and many other factors. What we have been attempting here is to single out one of these factors, which is at least of great importance, *viz.,* abstract temporal pattern itself, in order to make the nature of at least this one aspect plain.

As to the count of three instead of two in the first level of the grouping of beats in English, any example of the consistent use of so-called trochaic measure will exhibit the characteristic un-English sound of a strict count of two. Trochees substituted for iambs are not of this sort. From our scheme it is plain enough that neither *iamb* nor *trochee* properly names any actual unit of the temporal pattern of blank verse, for example, where prosodists constantly employ the notion of substitution as if there were a genuine metrical or rhythmical difference between measures which they scan in these terms of iambic and trochaic feet. The so-called substitution is possible because the feet themselves are defined partly in terms of the number of syllables, and so allow this breaking up of the measures of the line, quite without relevance to their actual metrical form; if, that is to say, metrical form is one aspect of the measure of rhythmical pattern. What else metre could serve to measure if not rhythmical units, one would be at a loss to know; though it is constantly urged that metre and rhythm are quite distinct, as if either the metre were the measure of nothing at all, or what it measured were not an aspect of the rhythm of the verse.

Not every half-measure of three counts in a blank verse line is marked by a heavy accent, any more than every whole measure is, either in music or in verse. In any scheme of prosody, as in any musical composition or any lines of poetry, the fact is taken into account that once a temporal pattern has been clearly defined to sense, only strikingly displaced accent prevents its being discerned as continuing in the form established. Typically trochaic verse, so-called, is a pattern where the lowest-level measure is an even two-count. All Americans, at any rate, are familiar with such verse as this in the *Hiawatha* of their early school days. Here we feel the perfectly un-English pattern of the almost mechanically regular *one-two-three-four, one-two-three-four,* or $\left(\begin{array}{c} \text{one - two} \\ \text{one-two, one-two} \end{array}\right) \left(\begin{array}{c} \text{one - two} \\ \text{one-two, one-two} \end{array}\right),$ no doubt felt by the author and his juvenile admirers as suggesting Choctaw or American Indian, and hence appropriate to the subject in a somewhat childishly romanticized version. Some *Mother Goose* rhymes have this pattern of measures built on *two's*. *Taffy was a Welshman, Taffy was a thief,* is regularly *one-two-three-four, one-two-three-four,* with each syllable of *Welshman* taking two counts, and *thief* taking either two, with two rests, or held out to fill more of the measure, with fewer rests to complete it. Jingles are sometimes easier to write than verse because they allow unnaturally heavy accent in marking off the pattern, and even accent on the wrong syllables, and the grouping of several syllables in much shorter time than normal speech would allow. But of course the classic jingles are classic just because they approximate natural English and simply overemphasize measured pattern by unusually heavy accent where the accent would naturally fall in any case. And this is a mechanizing of the pattern which gives a comic effect and a sing-song progress quite delightful to children and not totally devoid of attraction for adults. Such a classic as *Old Mother Hubbard,* however, is in strict three time, like most of serious English verse. She

goes to the cupboard to get her poor do-og a bone-two-

three-four-five-But when she got the-er the cupboard was

bare And-so on. All she does and all she suffers is properly trinitarian.

Perhaps the perfect naturalness of the count of three,
and not two, is best illustrated in the musical setting of
Drink to me only with thine eyes. Here the three-four
time of the music accepts accurately the temporal pattern
of the words as they would be spoken. The notes of the
song are held out to the full count instead of being broken
off for the slight intermittences of normal speech. The
rate in singing is also a little slower than speech because in
the music the single tones are pleasant enough in themselves to be dwelt on a little, and the pitch pattern that
they constitute is a further element worth a little more
time than the bare spoken words. But to sing the song
very much more slowly than the words would be spoken is
the surest way to lose its own proper effect. That is, instead
of being directly expressive, though a little sweeter and
tenderer for the simple flowing tune, the indulgence in a
much slower rate than that of the words as they would be
spoken, loses this very effect of words at their natural
spoken rate. This throws most of the expressive burden on
the tune, the actual character of which is partly just its
rate approximating that of speech. And the tune not at
this rate, approximately that of spoken words, has not a
pitch pattern of sufficient complexity to compensate for
the loss of the expressiveness of the natural speech rate. As

sung much more slowly it becomes banal and sentimental.

Elizabethan songs illustrate many stages of sensitive adaptation of words to music with such sure feeling for both as to allow wide departure from speech rates where the pitch pattern, including the harmonic structure, is in itself intricate and interesting enough to justify the departure. But the basis of much of what makes the songs of Campion so satisfactory to us even now, is perhaps more than any other one thing the feeling for the words themselves as they would be spoken, the sure expressive basis, disregard of which would be fatal to the intention. The settings of *My sweetest Lesbia, Though you are young and I am old, I care not for these ladies, Follow your saint,* all in rhythms of basic *three's,* will convince any one of the appropriateness of this count to the spoken words of the verse without the music, though of course these songs of Campion are not suggested as anything like *proof* of the contention that English speech uses this measure most naturally and most pervasively throughout.

In fact, no argument on the subject will serve our purpose here of showing that the temporal patterns we have indicated have been correctly discriminated. That these patterns are clearly discernible is plain enough; but many other patterns have been suggested, and some of them have been almost universally accepted at least verbally, though one may doubt whether the application of them has in many cases been actually to a clearly realized temporal measure and number. To find out whether the present scheme guides us adequately in reading classic English verse, we must of course recognize the pattern itself clearly, and then read verse into the pattern. If this falsifies the music of honest English, the scheme is bad. But so far as I can tell, the scheme is that which all of the sonnets of Shakespeare exemplify, with only such variations in detail as are perfectly usual in music and familiar to all of us, such modifications as do not dislocate or nullify the basic pattern of measure and number that we have made out, as for example occasional division into two counts where more usually the half-measures have three counts.

Vast amounts of blank verse, infinite numbers of heroic couplets, fall into this pattern of three measures to the line, each measure divided into halves, and each half further divided into three counts. The scheme never requires accents on naturally unaccented syllables, because it does not require accent all of the time to mark the measures or their divisions; it never requires substitution of one sort of foot for another, because its constituent parts are not feet made up of counted syllables. It is simply a temporal pattern of measures numerically subdivided. And it does not commit the obvious absurdity of dividing into five units—a highly cultivated late modern development—those natural, easy lines of English poetry which are called, on a basis totally foreign in its origin and its terms, iambic pentameter. If metre is the measure of anything at all, it is the measure of some aspect of rhythm, and the term *iambic* and the term *pentameter* describe no aspect whatever of the rhythm of blank verse lines. That rhythm has at least a temporal pattern not made up of five beats, or five measures, nor of ten syllables, but of three longer measures of the sort that we have indicated.

Thus the simple facts of the time order itself, and the equally simple facts about natural temporal patterns, do offer us a clear account of one essential aspect of verse structure, much neglected by literary scholars, and thor-

oughly falsified by many of the conventional prosodists
with their misapplied classical terms. And this would be
answer enough to the objection that general abstract æsthetic analysis offers nothing really interesting or significant
for our understanding of the arts because of its exclusive
attention to what are after all obvious elementary matters,
apparently beneath consideration for scholarly experts in
the arts, because they go below the established conventional
basis of what is thought of as genuinely relevant technical
study.

To give an adequate number of examples of the contention here as to the structure of verse in English, would be
to cite most of English poetry. But perhaps the conventional description of ballad metre as contrasted with its
actual temporal pattern is striking enough to be worth
citing before we leave the subject.

> Bid me to live, and I will live
>   Thy Protestant to be:
> Or bid me love, and I will give
>   A loving heart to thee.

This is one of those traditional forms where we should expect the simple, regular rhythm of a naturally divided
measure. If we scan the stanzas on the classic scheme of
counting syllables and naming and numbering feet, it
turns out to be an alternation of iambic tetrameter and
iambic trimeter lines, with a few substitutions of trochees
for iambs. What is mainly misrepresentative in this description is the suggestion that the lines differ in length
temporally and hence rhythmically. A simple check by
means of any ordinary reading of the stanzas will show at

once that the shorter lines are shorter only in the number
of counts that are filled with the sounds of syllables, not in
the measured time that elapses before one goes on to the
next line. The temporal pattern, fairly obviously, is of two
measures to the printed line, the division indicated by
fairly heavy accents. And in this pattern in time all the
lines are equal in length, the second and fourth lines of
each stanza being filled out with silences or rests so necessarily that in most cases it is next to impossible in reading
to skip the silent counts between the six-syllabled lines
and the following eight-syllabled lines. This is plainest,
perhaps, in the so-called run-on lines: the third of the
first stanza, where, although the rhyme emphasizes the
end of the line and thus marks it as the end of a measure,
we do run on temporally at once to the fourth line; and the
second line of the second stanza:

> A heart as soft, a heart as kind,
>   A heart as sound and free
> As in the whole world thou canst find,
>   That heart I'll give to thee.

Here the time scheme makes us go directly from the first
line to the second, though there is a marked break in
phrasing and sense, while at the run-on ending of the
second line, which calls in sense for the first word of the
next line without a break, we hold out the word *free* and
fill the last half of the measure either with this vowel or
with measured time empty of sound, unless we are to
break the rhythmic pattern completely.

The whole poem goes at a rate felt as breathless, and we
might be tempted to say that it was a case of two meas-

ures, of four beats each, to every line. But that the basic count is not two but three is perfectly plain if we try actually to divide the time scheme in accordance with our speaking of the words. An evenly timed *one-two-three-four, one-two-three-four,* for the syllables of each line, and the rests at the ends of the second and fourth lines, chop the stanzas into an altogether unnatural rhythm. An actual noting of the count that agrees with a rhythmical reading that fits the natural speaking of the words, gives us two regular measures of six counts to the line, grouped as follows:

$$\overset{1\;\;\;2\;\;\;3}{\text{bid me to}} \quad \overset{4\;5\;\;6}{\text{live and}} \quad \overset{1\;2\;\;3}{\text{I will}} \quad \overset{4\;\;5\;\;6}{\text{live Thy}}$$

$$\overset{1\;2\;3}{\text{Protes}} \quad \overset{4\;5\;\;6}{\text{tant to}} \quad \overset{1\;2\;3}{\text{be}-} \quad \overset{4\;\;5\;\;\;6}{--\;(\text{Or})}$$

The regularly occurring rests at the ends of the second and fourth lines in each stanza make a division of the stanza into two long lines, the fourteen-syllabled units recognized in traditional prosody. But in the time-pattern these are clearly units of four measures, the rests marking off the main pause in the rhythmical phrasing, and serving as the sole indication of this grouping of the parts of the stanza into two. For if the division depended on the rhyme, there would be no more reason for dividing the stanza into the two so-called fourteeners than for the division into four lines. Without the rests, in other words, the fourteeners here would not be indicated at all. The pattern, then, taking these rests into account, not as breaking the regularity of the pattern and the count, but as indicating by their presence a grouping of measures that puts the first and second printed lines together in one group and the last two lines in another, will be as follows:

¹ ² ³ ⁴ ⁵ ⁶ ¹ ² ³ ⁴ ⁵ ⁶ ¹ ² ³ ⁴ ⁵ ⁶
Bid me to live and I will live Thy Protes tant to

¹ ² ³⁴⁵ ⁶ ¹ ² ³ ⁴ ⁵ ⁶ ¹ ² ³ ⁴ ⁵ ⁶
be   Or | Bid me love and I will give A

¹ ² ³ ⁴ ⁵ ⁶ ¹ ²³⁴⁵ ⁶
loving heart to thee A

The very beginning of the poem illustrates a characteristic fixing of the count of three, very much as some of the

Shakespeare sonnets do: *When to the sessions of sweet*

silent thought, Like as the waves make towards the peb-

bled shore, They that have power to hurt, and will do

none, Being your slave, what shall I do but tend. Many
of the sonnets, too, fall into an emphatically announced
pattern—announced by heavy and unambiguous accents
on syllables—only with the second line, the first line
flowing like a smooth unpunctuated gesture, a sweeping
introductory stroke, the time of which is clear enough,
but the numbered measures of which take on their pattern
quite surely only as one reads into them the measures and
numbers of the remaining lines; the pattern becoming
pronounced and more clearly obligatory from the second
line on.

These examples will serve, I think, to indicate the nature of temporal pattern in its connection with rhythmical
structure in verse. They may show too that in so obvious
and simple an analysis as that directed upon temporal pattern alone, we find a scheme that leads to a more intelligent
grasp of structure in the subtle and complex art of English

poetry than would otherwise be possible. And this may serve incidentally to answer those opponents of analysis who feel less that our scheme is abstract and artificially complicated, than that its basis is so simple and obvious as to be uninstructive and, in actual application to the concrete compositions of the arts, irrelevant and useless.

CHAPTER V

RELEVANCE IN ÆSTHETIC ANALYSIS:
EXPRESSED FEELING AS FOCUS OF
INTELLIGIBILITY

THE preceding chapters have attempted to make clear the nature of analysis as applied to the simpler levels of æsthetic form. We have taken as a basis sensory elements systematically related in ordered ranges or manifolds to which they belong by virtue of their own nature. In this sense the elements are *intrinsically* related. They lie in serial orders intrinsic to their defining characteristics, and hence cannot occur except as exhibiting positions or relations in these orders. That is to say, when we consider certain aspects of relatively concrete sensory elements, the pitch of sounds (and all musical sounds by definition have pitch), the brightness of colors (and every color variation has its specific degree of brightness), we find the whole range of sounds or colors serially ordered with reference to these aspects of them. All musical sounds are in one single pitch series, as all the variations of color are in a single range of hues and in a single ordered series of degrees of brightness. And to hear a note at a particular pitch is to hear a note in its relation to any and every other note, as higher or lower than this other note by a determinate pitch-distance. To see a color is to apprehend a point in the range of hues related to all the other points in that range, to apprehend a degree of brightness and a degree of saturation determinately greater or less than that of any and every other color variation.

The elements and the serial orders or ranges are abstract in the sense of lying within one non-separable but clearly distinguishable aspect of the sensory content, an aspect of it which does not occur and cannot be present in experience except as integrated concretely with other qualitative and spatio-temporal aspects (as pitch is not heard except in an actual sound which has loudness, duration, timbre, and so on) but which can be imagined and conceived independently of these other aspects, just as they are discerned in and abstracted from such concrete composites in the first place.

We have noticed too that it is only in terms of the abstractly ordered aspects of sensory content that determinate controlled composition is possible. And it is consequently only in these same terms that a correspondingly relevant and accurate apprehension is possible of the structural forms actually given as æsthetic surfaces. Since, for example, in the ordered series of saturation, hue, and brightness, color elements lie at determinate color distances from one another, the juxtaposition of any two distinct color variations on a spatial surface serves to constitute the relation of color contrast between them in one or more of the series, a contrast that is directly apprehended as color design. This contrast is properly to be called structural—serves, that is, to constitute discernible form—in that it is not bare contrast, like that, say, which we feel between two contrasting smells or tastes, but a contrast of determinate degree or qualitative distance. It is a contrast in which in immediate apprehension the two elements are related more or less closely than any other two elements of the same sort or equally closely. They are related palpably in virtue of an ordered aspect of their own nature, related as two selected elements in a series, all of whose elements lie in this single order. Hence their relation is itself related to all the other relations in the series, and, as concretely exhibited, becomes necessarily and for direct apprehension a constituent of a structure when any other such elements are selected and added to the two constituting the original structural contrast.

The case is not roughly analogous, merely, but essentially the same, as that of spatial elements. In a given plane any line, in exhibiting concretely its own position, length, direction, or sequence of points, thereby defines these same spatial relations as constituents of the plane that it is in, which is made up of such relations. The relations exhibited by the line, being necessarily integral to this more inclusive structure of the plane itself, are integrally related to any and every other particular spatial element or relation in the plane that may be selected and concretely exhibited. In combination with such another relation or element, the line thus necessarily goes to constitute a more complex exhibited structure. For example, to take a very simple case, any straight line drawn on a plane will be related to any other line we may choose to draw in the same plane, in the structure called an angle, or, in the one special case, a pair of parallels. And this structure is immediately apprehensible as made up out of a combination of the relations exhibited or defined by the first line and those exhibited by the second, within an ordered manifold that is the plane itself. It is by belonging systematically in this manifold that the line is related to every other element of the manifold, and hence, with any selected elements of it forms a larger structure.

Exactly so of color variations and sounds. Colors are *in* brightness and sounds are *in* pitch just as lines and figures are in space. A sound, with any other sound, defines a pitch interval, because both are elements within the single one-dimensional manifold of pitch; and the two combine to define a distance measured along this dimension as a great or a small pitch interval. The serial ranges relating sensory variations are then the essential basis, the actual constitutive nature, of all sensuous structures. And so in a parallel sense not only of spatial elements, but of concretely exhibited temporal elements, durations of various lengths, whether of sounds or of motions, natively ordered in the manifold serial orders of space and the one-dimensional irreversible order of time.

Next we found how natural conditions of the occurrence of sensory elements having such ordered aspects, defined for apprehension patterns of selected elements in specific relations to one another, as measured within the serial orders, to which they allow us to give units of qualitative distance. These patterns too are abstract, and they are palpably elementary structures, discriminated or selected, and used by artists as foundational forms. Elaborations and simplifications, combinations and modifications of them, make up the more complex æsthetic forms of works of art, which are relevantly apprehended only as thus constituted.

We have also a little loosely, and for convenience, following a familiar and apparently significant distinction of common sense, classified patterns as of two kinds, one constituted of what we have called qualitative elements and relations, exemplified in pitch and the dimensions of color, the other of spatial or temporal or of spatio-temporal elements. It should however be clear that this classification is rather a concession to customary notions, which differentiate space and time from other aspects of things, than a systematic difference. In the sense in which pitch is an order of sounds, time is an order of durations of any qualitative content, and in the sense in which pitch is a quality, extension, whether temporal or spatial, is qualitative. Both are abstractions; but space and time are more pervasive aspects of the world than pitch, which is confined to the region of what is named as one qualitative realm, that of sound. It is within the abstract temporal order that we made out the general nature of the strictly temporal aspects of rhythm, illustrated in the measured and numbered patterns of English verse. Color scales and musical scales are qualitative patterns within qualitative orders, in the common acceptation of the term *quality,* as not extending to space and time.

But it must be clear that no work of art, even the simplest, is limited to being an abstract pattern. All works of art are concretely experienced presentations of sensory-imaginal content, where a great many aspects come together in a single object or æsthetic surface. This surface is not a blank qualitative datum, but a coherent structure with distinguishable parts in determinate relations, of course; it is not, however, *merely* an exemplification of some basic pattern or combination of basic patterns. When a musician composes he does not write out in ascending or descending order the notes of the scale. He puts these scale notes into an arrangement that he himself chooses, and a relevant analysis must follow his choice in the light of the nature of the effective whole that it results in. If we are to apply our analysis to works of art, it is thus of the first importance to see what guides the artist, whether musical composer or painter or sculptor or poet or architect; and this is at least more than either such basic patterns as we have discussed, or the more elaborate complex forms that have been built up out of them in the historical development of the arts, or been taken over from more or less complex natural or useful forms, either simplified or elaborated. For the relevance of the analysis of a structure depends on its being directed by what actually directed the structure which it seeks to grasp to its proper completion in a coherent whole, presented.

The criterion of soundness and relevance in analysis is much the same as the criterion of technique. Technical operations, whether in the arts or elsewhere, depend totally for their genuineness as functional technique on being integral to the achievement of a specific intention. For practice we may write sonnets or quatrains to see how words and ideas will fit into these historically defined forms, or chord progressions or exercises in the various species of counterpoint. For practice, a student colors a simple spatial design with variations limited, say, to three hues all at the same degree of brightness and of saturation. But these are exercises to gain familiarity with the sensory elements, with their ordered relations, and with basic patterns, as well as fluency and sureness in using all these to any purpose. They are exercises in grammar and syntax and usage and idiom in the various arts; but they are not what we usually mean by artistic composition. Such exercises are indeed works of art in the derivative sense, reproductions, with slight and sometimes even unconscious modification, of compositions or of structural units familiar to artists and often familiar enough to laymen. They may exhibit talent or taste but they are not quite works of art. They are not original but derivative in the plain sense that instead of taking their origin in an artist's own peculiar purpose, the purpose that defines activity as artistic, their function is the exhibition of a structure of a given sort, the exemplification of a definition that has been given by the works of others.

The purpose that *does* guide distinctly artistic composition, that makes art characteristically individual, and in that sense original as having its central determining source in its producer, is the artist's intention to express what he himself desires to express; although, of course, this may be fragmentary, the fresh expression of mere means to larger ends in more comprehensive works, but necessary to these new works as an adaptation of material and medium through technique to further ends felt as demanding such fresh means. Some of the work of very great artists is of this sort; and it is not a condemnation of Miss Stein, for example, to see in some of her writing a new kind of building blocks for other artists to use. But just what it is that an artist wants to do, just what may be properly and intelligibly said to be expressed, is still a confused and somewhat confusing question.

In language we usually speak of expressing *ideas*. In fact, most commonly the very meaning of the word *idea* is identified with what becomes articulate in words, and thus at least verbally explicit in conventionally intelligible sentences. Ideas are supposed to be proved to be ideas at all by just this process of linguistic formulation. If the formulation has any meaning, however, this is clearly not the words themselves; but either what they symbolize—com-

monly in imaginal and emotional content—to those familiar with the language used, or the cue to some indicated
response or set of responses. The function of a vast deal
of our ordinary linguistic discourse is nothing but the calling out of such responses, eventually in overt behavior. We
wish to convey to some one a fact or an explanation relevant
to a purpose or interest of his or of our own. We wish to
give directions, or to record an experience as bearing upon
a matter of common concern, to communicate this piece
of information to guide plans of action or to explain some
particular feature of the nature of things in general. Perhaps we wish also to indicate the conditions and requirements, consequent upon the facts or explanations that we
are communicating, for effective future conduct or for
controlling certain processes in nature. So far as we are
governed by such practical or scientific motives, conscious
or unconscious, our art of speech is strictly a useful art.
And it is only so far as a very different motive governs us
that our speech takes on an aspect that is characteristically
or significantly æsthetic. Artists and critics and theorists
are fairly agreed that this defining purpose of art as æsthetic,
the purpose of the so-called fine arts, is expression. And
anything that is expressed is at least qualitative experiential
content.

Actual qualitative content is always felt directly, not
merely discriminated and labeled; and it is felt with some
degree, however slight, of affective interest. There is no
concrete datum that is absolutely indifferent, because there
is no such thing as purely abstract conscious discrimination
in the sense of a separate process devoid of feeling; though
the results of the abstractly discriminatory aspect of actual
experience may be all that is relevant to theoretical or prac-

tical purposes. The world in all its actually presented concrete character, on the other hand, is more or less interesting to us, hence more or less objectionable or acceptable, liked or disliked. That is to say, the response to it is to some degree emotional. As our response is integral to the process conditioning the world's appearance in all of its aspects, so the emotionally conditioned or conditioning aspects of our response condition its emotional character. Hence its emotional character, its *feeling*, that is, the way it feels to us, is no less genuinely "objective" than its colors or its sounds, its shapes, its hardness, its presented spread and size; hence also no less objective than those units of measurement and those structural relations to which we confine our attention in the natural sciences and their symbolic formulations.

What is determinately presented is exactly there before us. And since we arbitrarily govern our bodily organic processes no more, and often far less, than we control the processes surrounding our organism in nature, the sense in which an emotionally satisfying or offensive presentation has its specific affective tone is just as determinately factual as anything could possibly be. To call it subjective in any significant sense inconsistent with these facts, is to attribute it to a transcendental conditioning not of the organism and the surrounding world, but of a very special sort of subject for which there is by definition no empirical evidence whatever. This subject, as we shall notice later, was inherited by the modern imagination from a dichotomy essential to Christian myths and mediæval dogmas. It was firmly established by the philosophical tradition of a metaphysics not content with evidence but clinging to the sole ground that would make of it an independent and significant discipline. At present it is the cultivation of a prejudice, philosophically rationalized long ago by Descartes, which takes the place of the religious myth and the succeeding theological dogma.

Concrete content that coheres in some single presentation to consciousness has a unitary qualitative tone, which is thus concretely felt. Such an object is not merely discriminated; nor is it merely classified in view of some selected aspect of it, which is taken as the distinguishing character of a kind of thing. Thus it is not so much an idea, as a whole concrete felt presentation, that even language—not to mention other media—communicates, when it is used for the sake of expression. It seems unfortunate that when what is expressed in art is called ideas, it is so commonly thought of as ideas in the sense suggested above of verbal formulation. For the nature of the meaning of such formulations has remained a sort of familiar mystery not to be discussed. But the whole cast of our training in a system of education through lectures and books has, in spite of laboratory science and pragmatic criticism, fed us so exclusively on words, that we can hardly help being satisfied with the very commonly specious explicitness of language, as if pure verbal content could furnish an acquaintance with anything but language itself, or for that matter, as if any other symbolism could have meaning and be knowledge without either presenting content other than itself, or referring to events and to the active processes of behavior. Even scientists sometimes grow to think that their conceptual symbolic schemes constitute the nature of the world, instead of being formal modes of intelligent relation to it, either by way of expert habitual operations upon it, or in the forms of diagrams presented as sensory or imaginal, which serve to picture it for our contemplation or to map it for our movements.

If we rule out its practical and scientific uses—the reference of language to ulterior action and its function in the pursuit of theory—and notice what language expresses in its more strictly literary function, particularly in poetry, we find that this is feeling or emotion presented as the qualitative character of imaginal content. And we should bear in mind that what is imaginal is not limited to being visual, however large visual content may bulk in almost all of our poetry. If it is asked how qualitative imaginal content can present feeling, how it can be actual feeling that art expresses, we arrive at the supposed miracle that art is so often said to be, the embodiment of spirit in matter. But thinking can have no intercourse with miracles. And since the simplest thinking finds that works of art do express feeling, we are forced by the obvious character of our data to look for feeling *within* presented content, as an aspect of it, that is, integral to its actually present character, or as its unitary qualitative nature as a whole.

The distinction of the spiritual from the material, when this distinction is taken to involve an actual separation in existence of one from the other, is so ancient and established that we are involved in an almost ineradicable confusion by bringing in the word embodiment at all. But we cannot remove the confusion without first recognizing it as such. Spirit is supposed somehow to be an independently existing thing which by its very nature is not body. And matter is supposed to exist apart from spirit and to be of a nature which is not spiritual. Feeling and emotion are taken to be aspects of the spiritual or mental life, while colors and

sounds, shapes and rhythms, appear as qualitative charac-
ters of material things or of physical processes. And no
one has more vehemently insisted on the low estate of the
merely sensuous than have artists and critics in their efforts
to uphold the cause of the arts on the ground of their essential spirituality. One might gather from what they say
that the reality of art is not sensuous content at all; that
the apprehension of the sensuous aspects of works of art is
even a distraction precluding the apprehension of their essential nature. It has thus become hard for us to realize
that the merely sensuous, meaning something that is solely
sensuous, is not anything that exists independently or appears in experience separately from other things; that, on
the contrary, it appears at all only as content for mind or
spirit. But more than this, without such content spirit or
mind would have no nature of any sort to characterize and
define it as anything at all.

What are so often called *mere* data, patches of color,
lengths of an extension, for example, are of course abstractions. This is nothing against them. It is true that
without abstraction such data cannot be discriminated or
thought of; but without abstraction there is nothing of
any sort that thinking can seize upon and manipulate. And
it happens that the direct having of experience is not what
is called thinking or what should be so called. It is not
discriminating and abstracting activity, however fully it
may be conditioned by such activity. It is, instead, concrete
feeling. And concrete feeling is feeling something that is
just there, present to feel, and taken in as a whole in apprehension. So far as attention can extend its grasp, feeling is
the full perspective absorbing the response of the organism.
Abstraction is involved in the fact that this perspective

itself is not the whole of everything, not the whole world, but just this perspective. Abstraction is involved in absorbed attention to a given content in two ways only, as its condition, which is previous activity making it capable of complete concrete grasp in any given case, and secondly, as the dependence of any such unification upon cutting off attention from other things, abstracting from the rest of the world the whole present concrete content. But the object of such attention is a total structure, with all its aspects integrated as one qualitative affective content. It fails to be the whole world simply because of human limitations in range of apprehension, not through human thought processes, engaged in non-æsthetic response to discriminate specific aspects out of the presentation and neglect the rest. This is the sense, I think, in which æsthetic experience is concrete feeling and æsthetic objects are concrete wholes.

An experience is æsthetic just so far as it is the full felt response to what is directly given (though given only on condition that there is the specific response as one of its conditions). Response is of the whole organism unanæsthetized, whether it is to be called spirit or body using its senses, which do not function of themselves but as employed by the organic mind, and which do not function separately from one another. With no response, no directing interest and attention, nothing is given at all, as we saw clearly at the beginning. But obviously feeling *is* given. Feeling simply *is* concrete direct experience. And if we were only free of the cultivated but factitious view that feeling is not defined in what is felt, but is in some mysterious way within us, and yet not "really" or "objectively" in our world, there would be no difficulty in seeing that the sensuous presentations of art directly embody feeling, that they are those bodies the presented nature of which is the presence of feeling determinately exhibited.

We may take up the matter a little differently, however, and perhaps make it plainer. It seems clear enough, for example, that we feel aches and pains and emotions as our own in a way not true of the smooth hardness of a table top, which is there for any one else to feel, just as its extension is there for any one else to measure; or of the slippery surface of an oyster that we put in our mouth, which we suppose to be like the slipperiness experienced by way of other mouths eating oysters. But what is the difference *in externality* between the feeling of tingling and prickling in our hand or our foot that has been asleep, and the tingling and prickling of carbonated water on our tongue? The comparison may be allowed perhaps on Max Eastman's authority, who gives it as an example of the poetically expressive use of language. And what is the most inward emotion but the feel of bodily processes, the mounting blood of anger, the inner sinking of fear? What is the coolness of water but the feel of it on our skin? What is the color of the sky but the way it strikes our eye, the way it feels through vision? It is the old story of the qualitative aspect of our world, which exhausts its presented character and content. This qualitative presence simply is the way the world feels to us through our senses as instrumentalities of conscious apprehension. Pale blue feels milder than flaming red just as definitely and accurately as it feels pale blue.

Qualitative terms are thus quite simply the names for the way things feel to us, approaching uniqueness of denotation with sameness of perceptual conditions, or in the other direction, with selection and abstraction in formal systematic contexts, accompanied by a symbolism articulated to fit the system of abstract constituents, elements or relations. Whatever is one individual thing feels just as it does and not quite like anything else, in the same way in which the figure two is distinct from the figure three. In mathematical calculation all we need is to have the difference sufficiently marked so that we do not take two for any of the other digits, whereas in æsthetic experience what is attended to is the full feeling of the one object we choose to dwell on. Even here, however, its unique nature is felt exactly in its differences, in constituent aspects and their precise mode of combination, from the features of other objects. And without training in discrimination the organism is not capable of feeling the unique quality presented.

At any rate works of art, in order to be anything at all, must possess unitary individuality of quality, must feel distinctively themselves to us, or else they are not apprehended as single things marked off from other things. It may be said that this is confusing two very different meanings of the word *feeling*. The sadness we feel on a given occasion is our own ineffable emotion; the notes of the funeral march are external sounds publicly external. But I think that we can show quite simply that this apparent difference of kind turns out, so far as æsthetics is concerned, to be one of clarity, simplicity, and determinateness, not one of the inner spiritual and the outer material, not a genuine separation between our own private being and possessions and the world's publicly available presence as not ours and not ineffable. For our own bodies are integral parts of our world; and all experienced content, no matter what the degree of abstraction and simplification, of systematic articulation and symbolic exhibition and concatenation, is ineffable in one and the same sense. And all of it is communicable in one and the same sense, though obviously in various degrees, depending altogether on human powers over media for pointing out exact denotations. One of the chief misconceptions of the arts is that they are vague in their expression instead of being the most precise modes of communication for any but the simplest and barest abstractions. These latter, in the sciences and mathematics, pass for having a different sort of definiteness, because in their extreme degree of abstractness there is less confusion and ambiguity, in direct proportion, apparently, to their meagreness of content.

One way to see this is the resolute attempt to apprehend any feeling clearly enough to control it. Say that we feel vaguely discouraged and dull. Whether we use alcohol or friendly talk to get our spirits back, to get back our feeling of freshness and satisfaction, our courageous vigorous mood, what we get back is just as accurately a felt state of our physical body as it is a state of mind, our mind being our organism as conscious. The physical organism actively functioning as a whole, and functioning at the same time consciously, is likely to be a cheerful spirit. Discouragement is complete only in suicide or at the conclusion of fatal illness. The spirit is the body as a living person, not a detachable foreign element accidentally tied to it for life.

Or take another example of a feeling or emotion that we think of as strictly spiritual or mental or internal and ineffable, and not physical, material, external and determinate. Take human love. The restlessness, the irritability, the extravagance of men in love is not, we say, the essence of love. Essentially love is a spiritual exaltation in devotion, not a bodily passion. But in fact love, without a material object present at least in imagination to define it, is not love at all, but solely bodily disturbance accompanied by so-called mental or spiritual unrest. This unrest, however, is the vague, incomplete consciousness of the disordered bodily processes. And as there is no clearly defined present object felt, so there is no clearly defined single feeling experienced, but a welter of successive transitory feelings only very slightly defined separately and not integrated into any one defined object of attention. We get relief from such a condition in mild cases by physical exercise or by turning our attention to something intelligible or habitual, a novel or a game of cards.

There is no determinate content for the feeling called love until the object of love is included as one term present and playing its part in the conditioning process upon which consciously present content supervenes. Then what was vaguely felt, uncoördinated, restless bodily processes, becomes in consciousness unified feeling of a determinate qualitative sort. That is to say, the response is now integrated and completed in an object that is necessary to its full being; instead of vague disturbance there is presented embodiment, whether this is the body of a person or the quality of a love poem. It is not a change in application of the term *love* when a poet speaks of his love as meaning indifferently his feeling or the person he loves. The present nature of the one is the present nature of the other, literally and accurately. What differentiates his feeling is the precise lineaments of the body of a human being, or the precise qualitative nature of any other adequate expression of that feeling in other media, whether poetry or music or painting.

To be in love is a long series of events and processes and feelings; the nature of any actual love is a unified qualitative presentation fully and deeply felt. And it is this presented nature of love that art gives us, not the process: the love of a mother for her crucified son embodied in sculpture, the love of Shylock for his daughter presented on the stage, the erotic passion of Tristan and Isolde satiating us through our ears. Love is a loose term for countless cases not too different to be named by one word. But what the word names is not, I think, an essential element common to all cases, but the determinate nature of any one case in a range of feelings, each unique, that are more like one another than they are like things which we label with other general terms such as wisdom or beauty or squareness.*

Or take a musical example. The quick rhythm and the bright sounds of a Mozart rondo are definitely not discouraged or solemn. They may even verge on the gay and irresponsible, the overt disregard of the insistent wretchedness and difficulty of living. And this disregard sharpens and brightens their loveliness, making it for Mozart himself, if we are to believe the quoted statements, the expression of actual anguish, the pain with which our sincerest laughter is fraught. The slow, heavy movement of a funeral march (literal slowness and literal heaviness or dullness in low-pitched, thick chords) is not gay, and may be extremely solemn. If we ask what degree of the grave or solemn, the despairingly sad, it expresses, we shall of course have to give specifications of feeling. But what could these

* The highly dubious and controversial theory of universals would of course demand an identical common element here. But I take it that modern nominalistic logic is at least as acceptable as Aristotle, and that in æsthetics, as in logic, one is not required to be an Aristotelian to be considered sane and even perhaps sound.

possibly be but specifications of tempo, loudness, timbre, rhythm, pitch sequence, and so on? These terms, applicable literally to the music, precisely specify the feeling. All solemnity is somewhat slow in time. Quick solemnity is a contradiction in terms; hence the feeling called solemnity is expressed at a slow tempo. And stately solemnity, sanctified to usage in the phrase *solemn state,* has heavy accents and well defined, even ponderous, movements, terms which again apply just as literally to the music as to some supposed spiritual essence of solemnity, which without such unambiguous and even measurable sensuous characteristics would have *no* character at all, no determinate nature, and would therefore be strictly and absolutely nothing, *i. e.,* meaningless. But such large general terms as solemnity, slowness, ponderousness of movement, will not do to make out fully determinate meaning or character. As love may be that of a father for a mature, distinguished married son, or that of a girl for her absent lover, or that of a mother for her new-born baby, dead the day after its birth, so sadness has not only kinds and degrees, but in every case its complete and precise determinateness as an integrated single feeling. We cannot specify even these kinds or degrees except in terms of the determinate objective presentations directly apprehended. Without being directed upon specific, determinate structures, feelings remain too vague to be said to have character or definition; and most of our names for emotions are large, loose covering terms for a great variety of feelings.

The presented objects need not be outside our bodies, of course. A toothache is a perfectly determinate and characteristic feeling, of its own unique degree, in any given case, of intensity and extent. It is not, however, an object ex-

pressed; for it has no intelligible structure that fully clari-
fies it to us, nor is it—and this is the main point here—
the conscious externalizing and completing of felt intention
by operations upon a medium. Artistic technique consists in clarifying feelings by means of such operations,
completing in external structural form an apprehensible
content. This content need be no more internal than the
tender pale blue sky or savage waves beating on rocks and
sand. But it need be no more materially external than the
clearly grasped rhythmical and harmonic form and content of a particular piece of music.

The point is simply that a feeling is never the feeling
of nothing. We feel *what* we feel, or we do not feel at all.
And what we feel, since we are conscious beings, is sensuously qualified content. Such content a toothache or
vague boredom has, as truly as the most expressive gesture
or speech or music or drama or painting or sculpture. But
expressed feeling requires as its object what an organism
with consciousness can grasp as distinct and individualized
and intended, the formal fulfillment of feeling, the vagueness and irrelevance gone, the response totally caught up
and directed in an object sufficiently complex to engage its
whole attentive interest. Hence the response has full emotional character, as well as the more strictly intellectual
character involved in discriminating structured content.
Feelings are feelings about objects, towards objects, *of* objects. While all that is needed to constitute an æsthetic
object is qualitative presence, no æsthetic object of any absorbing interest can be less than complex, while it must
also be sufficiently simple to be apprehended as *one* complex, its parts and aspects held together in one qualitatively
individualized presentation.

Significant æsthetic objects, such as artists are concerned to make and other human beings to appreciate, are on the one hand single qualitative feelings given in apprehension. On the other hand, they are intricate and coherent complexes of æsthetic elements so patterned as to constitute single apprehensible and exciting presentations of feeling, consciously requiring this embodiment to become completely and intelligibly any feeling at all, to become the intended full feeling only suggested in the artist's processes of experience and not defined until he has worked it out in his medium. The feeling is not constituted in its own proper being until the process is complete and the work of art finished. The work of art is æsthetically adequate to just the degree to which the apprehension of the constituent elements in the structure they compose, and present to a normally sensitive human organism, results in this concretely present feeling. In one sense, then, discriminating the elements is the condition of apprehending the particular determinate whole in question. In another sense the discriminated elements as apprehended in their structural relations constitute this whole, so that actually apprehending the qualitative determinate feeling is apprehending the constituents in this way.

It will be objected at once that clear apprehension of the spatial and colored surface of a picture is not getting its essential point, and is in any case not emotional but purely intellectual or perceptual, or even critical. The answer to this objection is now very simple, however. The adequate picture is one in which, if attention is focused on just what is presented in color and spatial form, and dwells on these as there before it, not explicitly comparing them or the whole picture to other things or to other pictures, nor distracted by any other concern, theoretical or practical, the natural attentive process, being intimately connected within the organism and totally directed by the presented object, will deepen into a unitary qualitative feeling, which is as clearly and fully emotional as it is intellectually discriminating. It is just as true that this feeling is the given character of the picture, as that the feeling is actually conditioned, both by the physical nature of the picture and by the organic emotional and other processes of the person appreciating it.

If, however, pictures were solely geometrical design and abstract color pattern, the feeling expressed in them would not be so deep as it is in most of what we know as painting. Various geometrical shapes have distinctively different feels, just as obviously as pale colors feel different from rich intense colors. But, as we have seen, the basic patterns of spatial design, and often of color design, are just as likely to be borrowed from nature's more or less elaborate forms as to be pure geometry or pure color combinations. And the forms and colors of faces and human bodies, trees and lakes, mountains and animals, cannot come to us without being felt as the forms and color compositions of these things. A low rectangle surmounted by a triangle is a house, a human dwelling, immediately apprehended as such, the strictly geometrical structure being intelligible and satisfying not because of our acquaintance with the forms of geometry, but because of our long and intimate familiarity with this shape in houses seen. And if the geometry of a house is secondary to its house-shape for immediate apprehension, it is still more obvious that the shape of a human body is clearly apprehensible scarcely at all as strictly geometrical, while it is quite thoroughly ap-prehensible as the familiar shape of the human body.

The content, then, when we are presented with such shapes, natural or useful, is directly seen and felt as these familiar things, or at least as the shapes and appearances of these familiar things. And no one who has lived in the civilized world can grasp a house in attention and dwell on what it presents to his eyes, without responding in some of the ways in which we regularly respond to the sight of a house. We apprehend the sort of shape and relative size that feel like a human dwelling place, warm with human comfort and affection, or bleak in abandonment, or sad in decay, or offensive in brazenness or dilapidation. And we apprehend its offensiveness as directly and simply, and usually much more definitely, than its exact shape and the details of color that mark, say, its dilapidation. Some of these formal details we must have apprehended in it, how-ever, if we apprehend the dilapidation at all. And unless we have apprehended all of them quite definitely, we have not apprehended this particular dilapidation, but only some marks that lead us to think dilapidation, or the word *di-lapidation,* as we already know these, and not at all to ap-prehend the dilapidation determinately before us in this picture, the character here expressed. In fact, so far as we have only noticed that dilapidation is here *represented,* we have not even seen the picture. We have missed precisely what is there expressed in its individuality, and substituted a general abstract label for a determinate concrete expe-rience.

It is this sort of non-æsthetic seeing that has so often led to the most irrelevant talk about pictures. What dull, tired tourists, with no special degree of sensitive response to color and line and spatial form, not to mention technical means to the ends of painting, made of the Sistine Madonna, was not very much of what is to be apprehended by full æsthetic attention to that picture. They saw what they easily recognized as a famous painting that they had heard of. And in the picture itself they recognized the Virgin and her child, the son of the God of their religion with his mother, and the obviously seraphic expression on the faces. What they dreamt of as they sat long before this shrine, whatever else it may have been, was least likely to have been the æsthetic content presented to trained vision. They took the picture as a presentation, clearly indicated in obvious and recognizable features, of the human nexus of their own religious faith, not as this particular one out of thousands of different expressions of that faith in painting, not as in this opulent and somewhat obvious Renaissance manner of a particular gifted man, using familiar traditional material to express his own prodigal facility a trifle blatantly. And "the greatest picture in the world" did not acquire that transitory status in nineteenth century America on any strictly æsthetic grounds of success in the expression of significant individualized feeling in an appropriate medium through a technique rigorously functioning to its exclusive and effective end.

The Catholic Church does well to employ its official sculptors and painters on the strength of their piety rather than their genius; art in the service of religion, all the sanctimonious talk to the contrary notwithstanding, is no more likely to be successful as art than art in the service of capitalism or communism. It is only if the artist is animated by something to express that his work will have significance or individuality; but both his technical artistic powers and the genuineness of his feeling are necessary conditions of adequate expression. The lack of the former is fatal to æsthetic adequacy; the possession of the latter is, for purposes of *representation,* often just as satisfactory as artistic genius. And once art is turned to ulterior purposes, particularly to representation, it is no longer æsthetic expression except by accident.

Training in æsthetic perception is the cultivation of habits that discriminate details so readily that their meaning, as we call it, is read off unconsciously and integrated in the larger but equally determinate effect that we feel as this individual expression of faith or this specifically presented case of dilapidation. *Full* technical æsthetic perception not only apprehends such qualitative character, but discriminates the technical and æsthetic constituents of the effect. And fully adequate æsthetic training would have the result of making us so familiar with the uses of lines and shadings, pigments and brush strokes, washes and masses, color variations and modes of applying varnish, that these would all be discriminated automatically, and viewed not separately but as they have contributed to, and remain integral in, the presented picture, which *feels* expert and subtle and strong, perhaps, as well as effectively desolate or warm or comforting or nobly religious.

Except for artificially dictated painting as practiced by unwilling students driven by any one of the scores of irrelevant motives that may make a human being into an art student for a time, or even for life, there is no conceivable guide to an effective qualitative feeling to put on canvas or embody in sculpture, except those naturally interesting feelings that suggest themselves in an artist's experience of natural objects and human events. These may range from the hard look of iron machines or polished brass railings to delicate shallows of light among grass stems, from feelings of the lightest gayety to feelings of fate and doom. But unless such sights and such human contingencies are interesting, that is to say, have a certain feel that excites an artist, it is hard to see how he could be impelled of his own accord to get the feeling out in a painter's media on canvas. What makes him choose one thing rather than another to dwell on and catch its precise nature is exactly his own feeling of it, which becomes definite and full only as he gets it expressed in composition. So that, although what is painted is very commonly called representation, it is plain that what is said to be *represented* is not the essential intention of the picture.

What the picture that happens to *represent* a garden wall with shadows æsthetically presents, so far as it accomplishes an artist's aim, is what the wall felt like to the painter, or what the painter felt as capable of being embodied in a picture with a wall in it. This may look not very much like the wall, in seeing which this particular felt effect was stirred in him, to reach its completion only in his picture; and it will almost surely look very little like that wall as seen by ordinary eyes. But if the picture is adequate to the sort of intention that defines a work of art, it certainly will put on the canvas such spatial and colored elements in such color and space relations as trained perception will apprehend to constitute this feeling.

In fact, only as an artist can see how his own feeling comes out in the actually presented elements in the relational structures that his medium provides through his technique, is he any judge of having accomplished his intention, any critical judge of his own painting. He may have at his disposal all the technical means that other men have discovered and taught. He has the world of nature and human experience to feel about him, and he has his own individual interest in the world, so that he feels particular aspects of it as more exciting than others, as all of us do. But unless he commands a medium and a technique in such a way as to select elements and combine them into an æsthetic object apprehensible through human senses as carrying the individual fresh feeling that he himself has had stirred in him by his world, he is not an artist except in the lazy sense in which we are all said to be artists because we have feelings, though we have no skill and no medium by means of which to express them, no art, that is, at all. Even language fails most of us on this score, except as genius has molded it to specific human expressiveness. And the poet, like other artists, depends not on merely conventional technique and media, but on so modifying technical means as to produce those fresh, genuine, and original feelings that stir vaguely in all men, but in the artist reach their consummation in technical invention and the artistic composition that may finally result.

Originality has not to be striven for. Each of us is original enough in being the origin of his own activity. But the integrity and patience, not to mention the physical and nervous endurance, that are demanded of any one who insists on being true to the exactly interesting aspects of his world of experience, who refuses to express the merely conventional and familiarly recognizable feelings of men in general, which like the rest of us he must quite honestly have to express along with the conventionally established ways of doing so, are rare among men. So much constitutes individuality and character in practical speech and behavior as well as in art. What is still rarer is, added to this patience and integrity, such command of a medium and a technique as can externalize the individually felt aspects of experience in individually distinctive, that is to say accurately expressive, æsthetic structures.

Illustrations are only too easy to find, and they prove nothing at all. But they may give at least a particular version of these general statements. Cézanne's trees, in one particularly well known water color, are indeed easy to recognize as trees, though not nearly so like, of course, as those of the same trees photographed. But Cézanne was not just painting trees. He was giving us the feeling of them with the spaces and lights among them, their fine delicacy in solid volume and space relations. This involves familiar outlines to some extent, of course; outlines not drawn, however, but apprehended in the contrasts of colored areas. And the water color gives this exciting effect, an effect not merely recognized as pale green trees with spaces and light among them, but felt sharply as just this look and feel of light and air and color. Delicate as pale green and lavender-blue are delicate, strong and clear as standing trunks of trees are strong and clearly spaced on the ground and in the air, intricate as shadows and lights on leaves are intricate, patterned as lights and shapes may be patterned in acute perception, complex and various and alive at every point like breathing, growing things in clear air; but all apprehended together as one single qualitative feeling, not nameable as lightness or subtlety or delicacy or strength or space filled with light and air and leaves and branches. Not nameable at all, except as the specific effect of this particular painting with its perfectly determinate degree of complexity, of delicacy, of color contrast and harmony, with just these shapes and masses and spaces.

Language cannot name the feeling here given; for language cannot reach, in these regions of light and color and volume, the specification that constitutes the quality of an actual, determinate, individual picture. The point of the picture, its effective being, is just this embodied feeling that we have, if with open sensitive eyes we look at it and let its character become the content of our own affective conscious life at the moment. If this could be as well translated into language, there would be no special reason for painting at all.

As Mr. Dewey has so fully and admirably shown us, the aim of art being expression, art is necessarily the nearest approach to anything like adequate communication. If we have not the faculties of perception and the emotional flexibility and range of artists, we are of course shut off from the last adequacy of appreciation. But communication is never altogether pure and undefiled. Moreover, the great artist is also a human being; and his own judgment of what he is accomplishing depends on his being able to apprehend normally and humanly, not what he may have intended, but his actual painted picture, the expressed embodiment of his intention as it is given to any human being to apprehend. In his talk he may completely confuse us and quite misrepresent himself and his work. That is, he may not be a poet, or, when confined to verbal discourse, even a reasonably clear teacher. But at the best, language could only hint at what is to be had through human eyes in color and shape and space and line. And our very need of the arts, their unique functional value, rests on their expressing—and hence communicating—what language cannot express directly in any case; for what language gives us directly is only words, conventional symbols, the meaning of which is to be found only in concrete non-verbal content.

Art in other words *presents* meanings. When an indirect symbolic medium like language functions æsthetically, it is in two possible ways. Completely familiar words in completely familiar linguistic structures are transparent. They are not fully heard but heard *through*. And we gather and remember their meaning accurately without at all remembering the words themselves. In fact, to put our attention so fully on the phrases used as to remember them instead of their meaning, often prevents reaching what they mean at all. When they are not heard but heard *through*, what they present is their meanings, not themselves. When language presents content by such transparent functioning, this content is not verbal at all, but fully imaginal and emotional. In the second place, words may be so placed with other words, not conventionally but poetically, and so integrated in specific contexts, that we find them in rhythm and in skillful connotation—which again is not verbal but imaginal—leading us to feelings which are not their meanings as separate words and phrases and sentences, but presented feeling, a content actually received by way of the sounds of words, the total meaning determined by both perceived sounds and presented imaginal content. Art is always concerned to present, not to represent, and it must be plain that when we are presented with a single content in experience, one and individual, this content is characterized by its felt quality, which is no more and no less truly emotional, and no more and no less truly intellectual, than any full concrete experience of any conscious being.

Thus it becomes obvious that analysis is sound so far as it is guided by the unitary effect that is the actual character of an æsthetic object. It cannot get on without the elements and the orders and basic patterns that are the common tools and the common property of artists for their constructions, as well as being the common discernible elements and orders and patterns in the apprehension of these constructions. But art requires also the discernment by artists and by those who are to apprehend their works, of the specific functioning of these in the particular whole which they constitute, their peculiar functioning in any given case in combinations only explicable and apprehensible in the light of the whole that they constitute. Analysis accomplishes its purpose in æsthetics only as all that it describes as elements and patterns are seen to be integrated in the effective quality or feeling that is the unitary æsthetic character of the given work of art analysed. And while much of this character depends on formal sensuous elements as such, the very nature of these forms, so often derived from nature and human experience, brings into art the non-formal significance attached to the same forms in nature and in life. The brightness or dullness of a color may then be integral to a design not primarily by virtue of its specific degree of intensity in a range of color intensities—though that it will necessarily have—but in virtue of serving to constitute the kind of a color design that is that of a smiling face or of pale, tortured anguish as it appears on a face. The formal function itself of elements and patterns is modified by their expressive function; for their expressive function cannot be exercised except formally. Everything in a concrete work of art is formal at one level or another, just as everything is formed content, and not mere form, on every level.

Analysis is as necessary for learning to apprehend works of art, and so to the knowledge of art, as the knowledge of æsthetic instrumentalities and expertness in technical procedure is to artistic composition. But both processes are guided by an end as intended by the artist and as grasped by the æsthetic observer, and this end is the feeling embodied in the concrete work of art. If it is a feeling completely foreign to our experience, we shall not be able to grasp the work of art itself as actually presented to us. And in that case our analysis would fail, because, not seeing what the constituents were constituents of, we should not grasp them in their functional relations to one another or to the whole.

The case is not unlike that of a statistical table in which we see columns of figures and other symbols, in themselves familiar enough and even arranged neatly before us, but totally lacking any indication of the purpose in the light of which they would have meaning. The parallel is not accurate, because works of art are presentations to sense, not representations of something meant but not present. But the senses too are instruments of our whole responding self, and they function to give us only the vaguest sensory data unless we have the organic means of correlating them into a whole. If that whole is a feeling totally out of the range of our powers, because it is conditioned by a complex of processes that we cannot attain even with the fully determinate physical character of the object to guide the articulation of our response, then our only help is to enlarge our capacities, to cultivate greater flexibility and range of perceptual and emotional apprehension.

And this we can do by learning accurate apprehension in simpler cases. A man who cannot hear distinctly the difference between a major and a minor triad may learn to do so by repeatedly attending to the difference between a major and a minor third. And so of color and space and time structures. So simple a pattern as a rhythm of two against three may at first be confusing; but a very little practice will teach us to hear this division of a measure in two different ways at once as a specific single rhythmical effect, as we all learn to see immediately the difference between a pentagon and a hexagon without stopping to count the sides. A complex pattern of polygons inscribed and circumscribed, a diamond in a tall rectangle, circumscribed by a hexagon or an octagon, makes a clear, easily apprehended design because all the subsidiary figures build themselves perspicuously into the more complex pattern, whether we see them thus the first time or are able to grasp the structure immediately only after practice in discriminating the constituents separately. In music an elaborate variation on a theme may be mere annoying confusion for a child or for any untrained ear; but the discriminating of the constituents by analysis will teach him first to grasp these separately and then to see how they go together, and finally, all this becoming automatic, to hear the particular effect of the particular variation in its own individual character.

When we know all of the arts in this way æsthetic analysis has taught us the nature of art. The case is not different when instead of a detail of sound or space structure, what we miss is the difference between a slightly ironic tone in writing and a matter of fact statement. A solemn, honest mind may be totally at a loss to see what the point of the words and sentences he reads can be, when these express an attitude towards subject matter foreign to his matter of fact naïveté, or to his honest, driving intention to understand what is being said. And the tone can be communicated only through subtler verbal differences, so that the only hope of comprehension lies in greater attention to these, until their specific subtleties are a matter of quick apprehension.

Thus the articulation of works of art, either by grasping technical means and procedures and their customary uses, or by discriminating æsthetic elements as such and the relations and patterns fundamental to composition in any given medium, will be the only sure approach to full grasp, when the total effect itself is not immediately apparent. Since, however, artists are human organisms expressing humanly available feelings, what stands between us and what they express is, in the case of contemporary artists, only their more gifted discernment and their greater range. A very possible stretching of our powers is all that is required to apprehend their works in their actual determinate character. We do not have to know the whole range of technical possibilities, or how to select from this range with sureness what an artist actually builds into his structures to embody the feeling that he is attempting to bring to consummation there. We have only to be able to discriminate the elements that are actually present through whatever technical means in whatever medium the artist has had the genius to choose or invent as best fitting his specific purpose. But unless we do apprehend all that is there in its structural relations as making up the total effect, we miss its fullness and often its main distinguishing individuality. Thus in pictures, and more strikingly in sculpture, we may apprehend little but a representation instead of what is actually expressed, and in music only a vague approximation to a general type of feeling, suggested in the scraps that we do clearly hear. All of Bach's fugues may be heard as containing themes, and may sound neat and finished, but not astonishingly various, nor any one of them specifically individualized or organically complete in clearly determinate feeling.

Analysis is a way of learning what works of art are in their actual presented being, by learning the æsthetic elements and relations which go to make up that being. And this would seem to be the function of æsthetic theory itself. The danger is, of course, that, failing to get any direct total effect, we insist on applying our analytical elements and relations and patterns as they might constitute some preconceived structure; as if, for example, we tried to relate the spatial elements of a Persian miniature in the perspective patterns of western painting and found it all naïvely incoherent. This would be failing to get its own effect and seeing only separate areas of design and patches of color composition, missing the individual distinction of the whole, and so not grasping the parts in their actual æsthetic function in *any* whole. And for all of the more highly individualized effects of works of art, their degrees of what we call moral or human, or in any sense deeply significant, qualities, this is not less so; the elementary discriminations of sense are the only possibility of the expression of these qualities, and not to follow them is to miss any chance to appreciate anything they make up. To suppose that the spiritual values may somehow shine out of themselves, unencumbered with the mere sense qualities, is to forget that without embodiment such values are simply nothing.

To judge works of art, however, in the light of our own preconceptions, would in effect be judging artists in accordance with the degree to which as original structural workers they failed and became derivative technical experts in the putting together of our accepted store of æsthetic materials and patterns. As we shall see, it is this attempt to judge works of art solely or even mainly as conforming to accepted structural standards, instead of apprehending them directly through keen perception and ready sensibilities, that leads to the disrepute into which criticism so characteristically falls. Not that criticism is as such useless, but that value judgments, if they are to be made at all, are not æsthetic understanding, and are irrelevant unless they follow such understanding. The practice of criticism is valuable only as its judgments are records after the fact. And the fact in question, if it is relevant, is the critic's adequate grasp of the artist's own means within his own medium carried out in the light of his own intention to the unity of feeling that his work expresses, whether from the critic's point of view this intention is significant or not. If it is genuinely and strikingly significant, it will be just such a unity as has never been achieved before, by means never used in exactly this way before. Hence it will not be apprehended quite at once even by the most discerning critic; and by the critic totally guided by historically established types of coherence, it may well be pronounced unintelligible, as to him it literally is. But this is not its condemnation, though that is what the criticism will no doubt purport to pronounce.

The adequate critic needs full acquaintance with all the traditional technical material there is, and with all the historically developed æsthetic forms and instrumentalities. But he also needs the readiness and flexibility, the freshness and range, that gives a margin for perception beyond the present scope of his controlled and surveyed field; for it is in this margin that any distinctively original creation necessarily appears. In any case æsthetic analysis as presented in these chapters, guided by the unitary feeling of specific works of art, appears to be the actual knowledge of works of art in general that æsthetic theory as such would take as its aim. And criticism and standards may be understood as an application of such knowledge to critical purposes.

CHAPTER VI

APPREHENSION AND CRITICAL
EVALUATION: STRUCTURAL AND
QUALITATIVE STANDARDS

MORE or less critical accounts of works of art make up so large a part of the available information on the subject, and critical estimates of the value of works of art have always held so dominant a place both in general discussion and in philosophical æsthetics, that it would not do to give an outline of æsthetic analysis without showing its relation to the practice and the so-called principles of criticism. That general æsthetics is not in the first instance art criticism theorists would of course avow. But they would usually add at once that though æsthetics is some sort of knowledge of a subject matter, it is not descriptive science, but normative. On such a view æsthetics studies not facts but values; and its principles, if it has any, are principles of value judgment, principles in the light of which we can see what distinguishes the positive from the negative, the good from the bad, the important from the unimportant, in art. If the theorist subscribes to anything but a flatly naturalistic theory of value, his æsthetics is thus a theoretical discipline that is not natural science made up of generalizations from data, but a set of principles grounded in something not to be found in empirical experience. On the basis of this, the good and the bad in the realm of art are to be distinguished. It should be clear, however, that any sound account of æsthetic subject matter would, so far as it defines the whole field, apply to the good and the bad alike, and that the distinguishing of them would not be its primary determining function or systematic concern, any more than organic chemistry would base itself systematically on the distinction between food and poison, instead of the general structure of organic compounds as such.

Æsthetic analysis, as its groundwork has been sketched in these chapters, offers explicitly no critically determining principles. In fact such knowledge of art as analysis would give, so far as its form goes, is like the knowledge that we have in any other science. Its content differs from the content of other fields of knowledge in the nature of the elements that are taken as basic, and the type of relations native to them, or to which they are susceptible. Its purpose differs in being limited to general acquaintance with qualitative presentations instead of with quantitative measures of processes. It is an account of the surface, and the surface structure, of our world, as felt in immediate content, instead of an account of processes conditioning that surface externally and internally, physically, that is, and organically or psychologically.

General æsthetics is a sort of qualitative mathematics. Its application to art is important and proportionately extensive, because in art the qualitative has taken on marked intrinsic significance for human beings. The qualitative is of course also the starting point of the most mathematical and logical aspects of science as well as the point at which all the symbolic calculations and equations of the most developed and successful science return to any application to the actual world that we are acquainted with. Logic itself begins in qualitative distinctions of this from that, presence and absence of content, assertion and denial formulated in abstract relations of implication, alternation, joint presence, and so on. Mathematics goes further with imaginative construction based on such simple abstractions and formulated in systematic symbolism. The natural sciences use these mathematical forms in an elaborate system of symbolic manipulation, which applies most strikingly to our world, perhaps, in the control of natural processes that scientific engineering has achieved. But in all this, while qualitative starting points are essential and qualitative results the sole possible indication of all consummations—whether in the felt warmth of rooms in winter and coolness in summer, or in immediately apprehended flashes of light of a specific color in electrified gases, or measured deviations of red rays discriminated by the aid of scientific extensions of sensory organs, and formulated by means of elaborate calculations—we do not in natural science seek as our final goal acquaintance with qualities and their own directly felt relations and structures.

We do use æsthetic data in all science; but we use such data as cues to understanding their occurrence, their dynamic relations, and the control of the processes which involve them; whereas in æsthetics we seek as our end a direct general acquaintance with content and structure as actually presented through sense. All this is of very special or of very great importance because in art, and in the æsthetic aspects of nature, such general acquaintance allows a fuller grasp of the character of particular works of art as apprehended, and hence the æsthetic appreciation of nature and art fully and accurately. Since art expresses in clear presentations through sense our feelings and the feelings of artists, the concrete character of the world of nature and life and human experience, it has seemed to men who took it at all seriously to offer us one of the main values of living, a satisfaction too great to be missed— if indeed there is any satisfaction at all that is not on some level æsthetic or artistic. But a science need not pretend to justify itself. If art is not of any great importance to men, then clearly neither is it important to cultivate æsthetics in those developments of it that have to do mainly with art. Only if we wish to have relevant and full knowledge of art in general, and of individual works of art in particular, is æsthetic analysis as so largely concerned with directly experienced qualitative structural content in art, a desirable pursuit.

But one of the most striking facts about art is that men like and dislike works of art with great intensity, so that they dispute fiercely and interminably over the relative values of such works and over the relative greatness of artists. A knowledge of art itself should make it possible to understand this, to see all this excited argument and hyperbolic assertion as grounded in the nature of art, which analysis is supposed to reveal to us. But if we take seriously our theory that art expresses feeling directly, but that it does so with unequivocal relevance to the specific work in question, only if the conditioning discriminatory processes of the organism are capable of ready and full response to the complex surface of the physical object bearing the felt æsthetic quality, then the enormous interest in art that human beings have shown and the violence of their conflicting evaluating judgments become clear. An enormous amount of the conflict is explained by the perfectly obvious fact that organisms differ. And they differ not merely in sensory discriminating powers, both because of natural aptitudes and because of great inequalities in perceptual training, but also in their readiness and range of perceptually controlled emotional correlation.

As we all know in these days, emotional possibilities and emotional clarity depend on a thousand details of individual development, from early infancy through the childhood influences of family, companions and surroundings, on through the manifold perverse possibilities of adolescence, the adjustments of social life, including those of marriage, and the whole range of educating influences, formal and accidental, physical and intellectual. We should not expect like responses to like objects from unlike organisms, any more than we should expect litmus paper to remain blue in an acid solution because it is blue in a solution that is alkaline.

But it is through men's common nature, not through their differences, that they know and serve one another, as Spinoza long ago taught. It is only by their like ways of functioning that communication is possible at all, and hence that science is a general possession. Æsthetics, like all other knowledge, makes its generalizations on the assumption that human organisms in perceptual-affective response are not totally various, but largely alike. Since the one test of communication is response, since response is affective as well as intellectual, affective content in any given case must be for all men sufficiently resembling to be amenable to generalization, if there is any full communication among men at all. Formal symbolic communication itself, whether linguistic or logical or mathematical, rests on this same basis. Hence if no æsthetic generalizations are possible, no scientific knowledge is communicable. The fairly obvious reason for our common view of logic and natural science as the sole fields of demonstrable agreement, compulsory upon men, is that most of science deals with extremely abstract specifications, with aspects of experience narrowly discriminated, unambiguously defined, thoroughly systematized in symbols and tested in operations, where again only these specific abstracted aspects come into question. And that logic itself is tautologous no longer needs remarking.

In æsthetics our objects are relatively concrete wholes, and our feeling of them is complicated by all that enters into a total organic response to the concrete presentation before us. Æsthetics has not reached the point where a fully adequate analysis of a whole concrete experience can be made out, partly because it has not been seriously cultivated, but partly because such an analysis would involve all the findings of all the sciences, a complete knowledge of the organic conditions of the response and a complete knowledge of all that there is to respond to, whether inside the organism or outside it. But so far as æsthetics goes analytically, there is no *a priori* reason why it should fail as scientific knowledge.

And there are theoretical compensations for its inadequacy. What we are concerned with in æsthetic objects is not primarily all the relevant conditions, but the structural whole in which they emerge as determinate content. It is within this field that our systematic analysis applies; if there were not some such boundary for the subject, then æsthetics would simply be science in general. And this is true of every other field of scientific knowledge. Since æsthetic content is by definition consciously present, its qualitative features may at least to a considerable extent be discriminated and analysed, without recourse to laboratory experiment or systematic symbolism. This can certainly be done on the lower levels of spatial configuration, melodic sequence, color design, and rhythmical pattern. In fact, so far as artists use humanly available technical and æsthetic materials and forms in their compositions, so far can other human beings discriminate through the normal exercise of their unaided senses, the concrete structural content presented, and feel its intention as intelligibly expressed.

Whether or not, or how much or how little men *value* what is expressed, will depend on a thousand details of circumstance and the countless complications of organic personality, as well as on accepted standards of value in many fields. But even human valuing is not so violently at cross purposes as the discussion of some theorists and critics suggests. It is a very rare phenomenon in the world when a reasonably healthy human organism, with ordinarily acute faculties adequately trained in perceptual discrimination, fails to grasp with some satisfaction what artists express in media directly available to such an organism. No two men will put exactly the same emphasis on laying aside some specific sum of money to meet future emergencies and normal expectations in a relatively stable economically systematized society. But this does not mean that no two men can mutually understand one another's financial precautions, though a primitive islander would need some training in a civilized economic community to know what financial precautions were. And it is such general agreement in understanding that we seek in æsthetics, not an impossible identity in degree of approval or disapproval, of liking and disliking in particular cases.

Although æsthetics is not primarily concerned with value judgments at all, it is plain enough that, taking as its subject matter the qualitative nature of objects felt directly and hence liked or disliked for their quality, valued in various degrees, it will, in giving an account of the nature of such objects, be relevant to value judgments, in the sense of indicating what conditions them.

Perhaps we have already indicated this relevance; but the matter is important enough for a little more explicit consideration. Æsthetic objects necessarily fulfill two requirements. One of these is that they be coherent enough to be single presentations. Otherwise they are simply not single things at all, not individual works of art, not anything determinate and distinguishable from other things. And coherence in works of art is achieved in many ways by many means. Always, however, it is through some sort of design or pattern, sequence for example, and increasing intensity and rate of occurrence of events to give order and form to a narrative, which reaches a climax, perhaps, and then recedes, by way of diminishing intensity of interest and frequency of new events, to a conclusion. The exhibition of a single character, recognizably a human being with human traits to define it, which may be made out in the most diverse incidents and places and relations to other human beings, will serve as well. Or the whole of a long poem may cohere solely in a particular feeling suggested, and gradually specified to complete determinateness, by the presentation of otherwise disconnected events, persons, places, situations, images of sounds and colors, broken sentences, unconventional speech rhythms, and even apparently perverse punctuation and printing. The most scornful critic of Auden's *Orators,* for example, is too familiarly acquainted with words and language, with sights and sounds and felt experiences expressed by language, to miss the unitary feeling that holds the poem together. And his condemnation of its formlessness, of what he insists upon as its unintelligibility, is wasted, since he himself points out its obvious coherence of intention when he notes this expression of clearly defined feeling in which it effectively culminates.

What we have been pointing out as the instrumentalities of art, and hence of æsthetic analysis, are the elements and the elementary patterns native to all controllable æsthetic material and involved in all artistic composition and in its apprehension. And the contention here is that it is combinations and complexes of such sensuous elements and such spatio-temporal and qualitative orders and patterns as we have surveyed that constitute any coherent form, however elaborate. The distinctive point of our scheme is that it starts with these lower levels, instead of being content to give rather vague literary names to the character of completed works of art, names which sound more adequate than our terms because they suggest the full character instead of defining particular aspects of the structure which has such character. Most of the famous traditional principles of æsthetics are of this large sort. Unity, coherence, a theme in variations, balance, symmetry, hierarchy, climax, simplicity, purity—all these are names for unification for apprehension, and also general characteristics of the apprehended object in its completeness. What we demand in works of art is sufficient coherence, however named and of whatever sort, to make a presentation apprehensible through sense, æsthetically present as some one object of attention.

If we are to have one large term to indicate this demand of human apprehending attention, this required achievement of unity, and to put it in a word that characterizes any or all of the kinds of pattern that could make a presentation structurally apprehensible to men and in this sense intelligible as an object of attention, the term *familiarity* is perhaps more instructive than these others. For what we demand is not merely a pattern or form—in the strict sense nothing perceived would lack some form or other —but pattern or form that is familiar enough to be grasped by us as pattern or form, that is to say, structure composed of discriminable constituents in apprehended relations. Nor will simplicity do, unless simplicity, like intelligibility, is equated with familiarity. Many a configuration difficult to grasp as geometry is eminently simple and clear geometrically, as compared to the pattern of a human face or a human body; but we have become familiar with this extremely complex configuration; we find it an intelligible form because we have learned it and know it.

So of most of the other traditional terms listed above. None of them is of much actual help in gaining a sure acquaintance with works of art and the nature of art in general. What we require is a prior acquaintance with the more fundamental lower-level patterns discriminated and familiarized by perceptual training, elementary spatial, temporal, and qualitative relations and structures out of which all the more complex patterns are composed, to become, under names suggestive of the quality of the whole, its purity, its unity, its thematic consistency in variation, its simplicity and its balanced symmetry.

Apprehensibility, however, based on familiarity is only

one aspect of what attention demands in any æsthetic object. The second requirement is that of interest, which amounts in one way or another to the demand for novelty. If unity is to give us satisfaction in art, it will be because it unifies something. It is the variety that is held together in it that gives it any concrete content at all, any actual being. The absolutely unitary is nothing. Nothing actual is unified except as constituted of the various. Abstract order itself, order as such, being by definition the order of nothing, cannot even be present to sense. And æsthetic objects by definition are so present, whether in perceptual or imaginal sensory content. They are the actual being of what is affectively and imaginally perceived. So of the absolutely pure, the absolutely coherent, the absolutely formal under any name. These large terms are meaningless as describing works of art unless they are taken with their complementaries, variety to give content to unity, sensuous richness to make purity not a mere blankness, complexity to give simplicity apprehensibility at all, novelty to give interest to the familiar, to make familiarity anything but inattentively felt dullness, to keep æsthetic content from degenerating into mere cues, æsthetically negligible, though essential to the habitual and scarcely conscious expert response that is characteristic of theoretical and practical activity.

Now different men will be more or less interested in different sorts of content, as well as varying in their capacity for grasping different sorts of form. But all men take satisfaction in clearly apprehensible presented structure, if there is any content in it to interest them. No one can remain alive in the world and not have feelings; and no feelings, as we have perhaps clearly enough seen, can be fully present and determinately characterized except by their affective-sensory qualitative natures. We might live in the dark regions of incompleted impulse, at the mercy of subconscious organic processes never expressed or possessed, but always possessing us in the disordered flux of what is often taken for spiritual life, though it is coming more and more to be seen as mental-bodily disease, commonly eventuating in melancholia or some other nervous obsession. We might live in this morbid content. Or we might attempt to abandon all sensuous or qualitied content in a habitual activity, not so much like that of full human consciousness as like the perfect social behavior of ants (if ants *do* behave without individual feelings and æsthetic pleasure). We might in our lust for action and control become more and more like the complex and accurate machines that excel scientists and engineers themselves in fineness of discrimination, expertness of operation, and tireless continuity of action. But unless we are to live in one of these inhuman ways, we shall be marked as human by being æsthetically attentive to what interests us in our direct experience, our apprehension of the qualitative affective-sensory surface of our world.

It is only elementary sanity to realize that our interests, of which we are usually not at all consciously aware, and which we never totally control, guide our selection in apprehension. It is equally clear that adequacy of apprehension will be facilitated by such interests, and that interest may also center on formal apprehensibility. It is only natural, then, that in seeing and judging works of art, even the most adequate critic depends largely on his own store of known structural forms, gathered under the guidance of his own interests, and available to his own emotional capacity.

These forms will be not only elements and elementary patterns, but also the complex developed patterns that have become familiar to him in his acquaintance with the art of the past. The intelligible will thus be defined in terms of the forms with which he is familiar, and the interesting in terms of the sort of thing that has already interested him. But of course the only authentic motive for artistic composition is individual feeling, originating in the artist, to be externalized. Unless in the process of externalization, which is the actual constituting of the feeling determinately, the artist uses sensuous elements with a consciousness of their intrinsic relations and their structural possibilities, he cannot even be controlling the æsthetic structure he makes. For these relations, being intrinsic to the elements, will of necessity appear in his work and make up its actual character. But the materials an artist works with include vast ranges of patterns already known through their previous exhibition in works of art, fundamental patterns like that of the scale in music, and the simpler geometrical figures, as well as natural forms selected out of experience at higher levels of structural development. And it is in terms of these, as well as of elements and intrinsic orders, that he works consciously. It is therefore these that apprehension must discern in his work if this work is to be grasped at all as what it actually is.

Thus critics require familiarity with patterns at all levels of complexity if they are to be able even to see what is before them. But no such knowledge will give them the individual character of a genuinely original expression in art; for it is the very nature of such expression to mold instrumentalities to the fulfillment of a unique intention; and important artists are marked by the degree to which such molding of instrumentalities to fresh purposes takes place in their work, as truly as by the individuality and significance of the intention itself. New feeling, really felt, becomes determinate only in new form; for its nature is new and individual, and this nature is exhibited in the form that its content takes on.

What are called critical standards are very largely the structural patterns of works of art that have become familiar to critics. It is clear that without such standards neither critics nor any one else could apprehend such works in their presented nature. But to apply these standards not for purposes of discerning what is presented, but to judge its value, is clearly misleading. To apply the specific complex elaborated pattern of a Greek play to anything that happens to call itself a play, to find this pattern not exemplified, and upon this finding to condemn the so-called play as either not a play or not a good play, is irrelevant pedantry, not authentic criticism. What it purports to criticize has perhaps not even been discerned. The critic has thought of and mentioned features that are not present in it, and he has also thought of a structural pattern that it does not fit, and that therefore does not fit it. So far he is of course correct. What he says is an account of what has happened to him when he was faced with the play and put his mind on something else. But the irrelevance of his pronouncements to the play itself is patent. And the amount of criticism that is of precisely this sort is very great indeed. The remark that the critic can justly make in such circumstances is that in its general form, or in various particular features, what is before him is not a Greek tragedy. But if it is a modern play, it is hard to suppose that any one would have expected it to be. A modern play is as a matter of course not a Greek tragedy. No modern play could be a Greek tragedy. And if not, then there is no particular feature of it, no general pattern constituting its form, that would sanely be expected to be that of a Greek tragedy.

If it is objected that to be a play at all requires fulfilling the definition of a play, the answer is in the first place that if there is any such definition, it is necessarily in very general terms, only the specific determinations of which in a given case constitute the pattern of any actual play. Individual interest and expressiveness are no more determinately definable in the broad terms of a general definition than is the specific individuality of a painting definable or exhibited in the fact that the main figures in it roughly make out a triangle, or that it consists in a spread of colors over an appreciable area. In the second place, what specifies any æsthetic composition in its individuality is, as we have seen, the unique feeling expressed by it. It is this determinate feeling that is its own peculiar being; and no determinate feeling can possibly be defined in the general terms naming the general characteristics of all plays. In the third place, such general terms taken together make up a definition of a genus or a species, and to suppose that there are any such entities as these, complex universals common to many individuals, not only involves us in an extreme and highly dubious form of ancient and generally repudiated doctrine, but forces us, if the notion is to apply in æsthetics, to consider such a universal present to sense. This is a palpable impossibility, however, since universals of genus or of species could not on any theory be presented sense content. The fact seems rather to be that we distinguish our experiences in the first place by their marked differences from one another, not by an identical common character, and that the various contents experienced differ in widely varying degrees. For convenience we group together things not too greatly different from one another, and then use a general name, which we apply indifferently to any member of the group, but which does not name an identical character to be found in every member of the group or in any one of the members.

Even if the abandonment of such antiquated realism in other fields were too shocking to minds habituated to the convenient fiction of identical common natures as necessary to give meaning to class names, and so also to general adjectival terms, which are in fact quite another matter, it is plain enough that in æsthetic theory we cannot arrive at the individuality of any particular work of art by any definition that fits anything else. And since this unique individuality not only constitutes the essential character and hence value in works of art, but also furnishes the only authentic guide to relevant analysis, it should be fairly easy to see, not only that the assumption of a common defining nature in them is highly dubious, but that the fact that they exemplified such a common nature—if this *were* a fact—would be quite beside the point, so far as insight into their actual felt character is concerned. So much Croce long ago established beyond any reasonable doubt, even if his more general denial of the significance of species and types in art is less easily acceptable.

Without ready apprehension of a great number of

particular forms and patterns, without a knowledge, that is, of the structural constituents of artistic structures, no one is prepared to apprehend what any work of art of the least complexity presents for apprehension. But whether or not a work of art uses one or another sort of constituent pattern, has little to do with its expressive character, except as such constituents do or do not serve to fulfill and specify the artist's individual intention. And the form of the whole, if the work of art is genuinely expressive of anything original, that is, of anything individually felt and intended, can never be experienced and so known to critics, until they have found just this uniqueness. Hence to have a store of definitions and patterns, no matter how structurally adequate these may have proved to be in other cases, and to use their non-occurrence as constituents, or their non-exemplification in the whole, of any work of art, as a criterion of its value or an account of its presented character, is plainly fatuous. And that this is the very common practice of informed critics—possible to them because of their solid training in materials and technique, and their wide acquaintance with historical examples in the arts—is abundantly proved for us in the abusive caricatures, by way of description, of original works of art in every generation, and the successive condemnation by good taste and authoritative criticism of what have been accepted later as the most significant creative schools of art and the most important works of the greatest individual creative artists.

If, however, critics who have generous knowledge of the arts and an informed interest in the work of artists, reverse one another's judgments or even their own, with the passage of a few years, it is plain that when ordinary mortals put their attention not on apprehending what is before them in works of art, but on expressing their more or less irrelevant feelings in the presence of these works, and then pass on, on the strength of this, to judgments of their relative value, not only do they express conflicting feeling and judgment, but the conflicts that they express have nothing to do with the character, much less the value, of the works of art that are purported to raise these issues.

Such activity helps neither themselves nor any one else. Quite the contrary. For it precludes analytical discrimination of what is there to apprehend, and, if must be, to judge. It is no help towards acquaintance with the work of art in question or towards greater knowledge of the nature of art in general. Our dominating personal interest in having and expressing feelings of our own, instead of submitting ourselves to the feelings presented to us by others in art, by way of ready apprehension based on perceptual-affective training, stands in the way of our enlarging our range and scope. We actually refuse the proffered communication of other men's feelings, and most violently and abruptly and with least consideration just in those cases where the communication would be of fresh and stimulating content, demanding that greater variety of processes in us that is the development of vitality. We refuse to take on those various rhythms and motions, to achieve the aptness of body and mind that are their increase towards perfection, their only rational happiness. And the confusing conflicts introduced—not into art, of course, but into more or less irrelevant discussion and criticism that purports to concern itself with art—when such self-indulgent and short-sighted egotism is substituted for appreciative apprehension, may well lead a novice to despair altogether

of soundness in æsthetic theory or to compensating cynicism. But such cynicism, directed towards art itself or
towards æsthetics, has its actual ground in thoroughly
irrelevant data, supplied by such professed criticism and
such heated and misdirected discussion as we have just
been considering. And its object, like that of the criticism
of the Christian religion at its lowest ebb in priestly and
papal corruption, should be those who furnish the data,
not art or religion or æsthetic theory.

To notice such irrelevant use as this of structural patterns, taken as criteria of taste and of value in artists and
their work, is not, however, in the least to object to the
relevant use of these same structural patterns or standards
of composition. And it is very far indeed from a denial
of the being or the significant function of standard structural patterns and their absolute necessity to apprehension.
It must, on the contrary, have become clear that without
such structural patterns to apply as norms, apprehension
is helpless either to discriminate structural constituents or
to apprehend qualitative structure as a whole and as concretely given. One further example may perhaps make the
point more convincing and indicate the literal necessity
for elementary patterns, to serve as norms for so much as
acquaintance with the actual character of any work of
art.

A great deal of what is generally accepted as the most
adequate and satisfying sculpture that has been produced in
the course of human civilization uses the human body as
its dominant theme. Most of us nowadays do not see the
human body regularly as part of our surroundings, unless
we live at the seashore and spend most of our hours on
the beach. And we have only recently emerged from a

dark period, which obscured the body not merely by covering it from physical sight with clothing, but also by erecting a thick screen of fantastically perverse moral sentiment, which averted from it the eyes of the mind as well; so that no full attention to its form was possible in open, untrammeled apprehension. Sculpture in such circumstances was hardly itself, and certainly not adequately seen or appreciated. To the apprehension of a man brought up in the late 'nineties in the United States, the normal, and certainly the only proper, form of a woman from the waist down was a truncated cone spreading to a wide base on the ground. The female nudes of art galleries presented to his eyes forms so strange in respectable public places that he had to get over the sense of an indecent exhibition of nakedness before he could even see what was actually presented to his eyes. Even then the forms seemed distorted and unnatural. That they expressed nothing but the lure of the flesh in highly sophisticated form appeared obvious, as apparently it does still to many an honest and benighted citizen, especially those interested in the moral well-being of the rest of us. And so also of sculpture.

But whether our preconceptions are thus blinding or not, it remains the fact that only the possession in imagination of some pattern of the human body, gathered from experience, can furnish the required preparation for seeing the specific shape of any human form in art. The bare spatial proportions themselves are indeterminate without a pattern by which the eye can measure them, as any one can demonstrate to himself by attempting to name any spatial feature of such a form presented. Is the torso slender? Only, of course, in proportion to the dimensions of other parts of the body. But what is this proportion?

Exactly what from experience one has gathered it to be. Such a norm we must possess, if there is to be anything in what we see determinate enough to be describable in any terms. Is the neck short and stocky? Only in proportion to other features in the first place. But any neck is short as compared with the arm of the same figure. Thus we require a set of normal proportions held in mind, if we are even to see the specific features in their determinate character. And without such character they are obviously not the particular features of the form actually to be discerned.

This discernment of spatial form and proportion goes only a little way towards the apprehension of the expressive character of a sculptured figure. But how definitely essential this preliminary seeing is to full apprehension is plain enough. The Greeks clearly realized it. If not, the formulation of a canon such as that of Polyclitus becomes meaningless. But the Greeks were tempted—as the whole Platonic theory of forms shows plainly enough—to look for perfection in the canon itself; and the Egyptians went so far as to reject as not even permissible in art any deviation from their canon, which was sanctified and stabilized by priestly authority. Since no abstract spatial pattern gives the last specification to the determinate contours of a particular figure, there was still room, however, for some degree of imaginative play and for some individual satisfaction, as well as individual expression, in concrete technical completion. When sculpture is free expression, however, what is expressed comes out only by virtue of the underlying structural orientation of parts—head above shoulders, torso above legs, legs tapering downwards, and so on—and the normal proportions of the parts, to give specific felt character to the features and to the whole. What is thus presented is not only slenderness or delicacy or strength or great stature, but such more complex and emotionally characterizable states or attitudes as breathless excitement, or vitally alive repose, or any one of innumerable other human attitudes and sentiments that may be specified in the modification of the norm to a unique individually expressive sculptured figure.

To feel the abnormally long bodies and faces of El Greco as merely distortion, instead of feeling them as ascetic and in some of his portraits as aristocratic, or as expressive of saintly ecstatic emaciation or intense religious striving or straining, or as whatever more specific and concrete embodiment of feeling any one of them is than is expressible in these indeterminate words, is not only to miss the point of El Greco's painting, but in principle to miss the point of the arts as expressive and not merely representative. It is often equivalent to seeing in art only the attempt to reproduce either a normal pattern or a particular physical object; and sculpture has probably suffered more than any of the other arts from this mistaken notion of its function. Or rather, it is with respect to sculpture that *we* have suffered most, and lost most, by our disingenuous or confused or naïve attempts to find in it something much more obvious and less significant, something much more easily grasped and judged, than any expressive sculpture could be. This is partly due to our lack of familiarity with its underlying norm, so that expressive and sensitive modification of that norm was not even apparent to us, and partly due to the lack of anything but the one theme of the human body in so much sculpture, so that there was no extraneous incidental interest to take our attention, as there is in painting and still more in architecture. In much of the nineteenth century we lost even the discernment of its spatial character as such on account of our irrational refusal to be perceptually acquainted with its underlying norm.

Sculpture is thus a striking case of the way in which the lack of perceptual training in the simplest sorts of discrimination, and in acquaintance with even the most available natural patterns and details of form, results not only in a lack of æsthetic sensibility and relevant appreciation of art, but also in plain sensory blindness and crude ignorance. And this is an ignorance of the actual concrete nature of the world we live in in conscious life, the world at that degree of qualitative differentiation that is apparent from the point of view of the normal human senses. It is this sort of ignorance that the practice of æsthetic analysis might help to dispel, along with the strange delusion that the world from some more microscopic point of view or by way of some more broadly inclusive angelic or divine type of apprehension is more real than the world that we find about us. This involves the fallacy of separating appearance from reality, not as the distinction between one way and another in which whatever there is may appear to beings of different degrees of power and fineness in discrimination, but as the difference between the spurious and the genuine, as if the genuine could be anything but one kind, fully characterized from some point of view in some sort of perspective, as distinguished from some other kind. And to call one point of view real, and others not real, is to deny the obvious fact of the actual variety of perspectives that our own experience acquaints us with.

This sort of ignorance of the actual concrete nature of the world that we live in in conscious life is likely to be condoned, simply because the knowledge that would remove it is so available and potentially so common a possession. But it is a little stupid of us to forget the function of æsthetic theory in enlarging and refining and systematizing every-day knowledge, just because it happens that the word æsthetic has a connotation in which, quite properly, its relevance to art is most emphasized. It is stupid, too, to rest content in such unnecessary ignorance of the actually present features of the world we live in, simply because we are willing to forego any full acquaintance with the arts and their nature, rather than think of ourselves as belonging to a region inhabited by æsthetes and filled with esoteric distortions of no use in a normal, healthy, practical life.

It is our lack of perceptual discrimination and training in general, our superstitious belief in language and symbolism as the sole instruments of knowledge, that so largely turns these instruments into ends and allows us to feel informed and even wise, not to say learned and scholarly, when an enormous proportion of our wise information and our scholarly learning is verbal and symbolic content or some facility in linguistic activity and symbolic manipulation. It is as if training our larynx to the automatic ejaculation of the syllables of some language, preferably a foreign one now no longer in use, were on some ground more genuinely an exhibition of acquaintance with the world of civilization than the automatic fluency of our fingers on a keyboard, running through the phrases of a piece of music. The difference is more likely to be mainly that in one case there is little structural content as sound pattern, with a pretty vague and in all probability un-authentic meaning beyond, whereas in the other the sounds are quite fully structural in themselves and thus constitute the direct presentation of given felt meaning, and so of an actually determinate aspect of the world of civilized experience. And that men should, as we so largely do, think of themselves as tolerably educated when in the whole region of sounds and colors and shapes and forms in general, we are as hopelessly lost as are children of two or three years in the regions of language and mathematical symbolism, is one of the anomalies of our times. Moreover it is not true of the ages that we all extol as great. "Taking the prospect" or following a musical score was as ordinary an occupation for Evelyn in the seventeenth century as making a financial calculation or operating an electrical device is for us today. And one may suppose that men of education in Greece in Aristotle's day, in Florence of the Renaissance, and in the London of Elizabeth did not avoid elementary acquaintance with the arts as beneath them.

It is not as if there were two worlds, one known through linguistic and scientific symbolism, the other through the senses and indirectly through symbolic systems. These latter are empty and meaningless unless they communicate exactly such discriminated aspects of the sense world, or such sensuous structures, as æsthetic apprehension gives us in the arts. Unless, of course, the linguistic and scientific systematic symbolic forms remain simply such complex structural imaginal content as the symbolism itself directly presents; in which case the symbolic systems and forms are quite obviously the works of one of the more esoteric arts, and acquaintance with them is no more truly knowledge or learning (though of course no *less* truly) than acquaintance with the red of a rose or the sound of the simplest nursery song.

Even the study of the arts themselves is only too easily turned into the cultivation of purely practical skill in manipulation—like so much of laboratory work in the sciences, where we spend hours in learning to seal heavy glass tubing over a gas flame, or to boil liquids without breaking test tubes and glass beakers—or it becomes the sort of verbal expertness and verbal memory that never misplaces the most minor name in the history of painting, never confuses the terms entablature and pediment, can recite a list of artists in any field in the order of their greatness as pronounced upon by the authorities, and so on and on. There is required no necessary feel of the difference between the lines of one draughtsman and another; verbal fluency on the subject of tempera, fresco, and oils and varnishes need never be interrupted by an inkling of the specific effective actuality of the look of any one of them.

These are of course extremes of irrelevance. We have at the opposite extreme such relevant analyses as Mr. Tovey's of musical works and Mr. Barnes's of French painting, though these are at such high levels of both learning and taste that for most of us they offer directly more verbal sophistication than actual acquaintance with the works analysed, unless we are extraordinarily well prepared for them by the elementary knowledge that æsthetic analysis on lower levels would furnish. We have also the lonely devoted teachers of the arts, who refrain in their instruction from exhibitionism even indirectly through performances by their pupils, as well as from verbal emptiness or the imparting of mere operative skill. But there is so little general understanding of the arts in our men of science and learning, and our masters in education itself, that all but the "authorities" in art and æsthetics on the one hand, and the virtuosi on the other, are likely to be quite unknown as forces in education, their competence or incompetence lying in a field where the ignorance of the learned leaves them free play upon helpless younger minds for good or ill. And those who harp upon standards in education are likely to be perfectly ignorant of the nature of the arts; while those critics and theorists who insist upon *critical* standards in the arts themselves, are often contentedly ignorant of the nature and function of the actual structural patterns and forms that constitute these standards.

But critics have another set of standards, not of the structural sort that we have been discussing throughout, which are often explicitly applied for descriptive purposes as well as for the purposes of evaluation. These appear usually as the names of qualities and degrees of qualities.

There are many qualities generally felt as desirable or undesirable, the names for which, even when they are used for description as literally and accurately as possible, have a definite value connotation. To apply to the harmony of Brahms in certain passages the term *thick,* is taken to be a disparaging comment, though thick foundations as such are not necessarily objectionable. The term here is simply a loose characterization of certain aspects of structure that more adequate analysis would put in more determinate form. Many of our critical descriptive terms are like this and are acceptable enough as rough designations at once of structural character and qualitative nature. But many other terms, such as sweet or harsh or brittle or flowing, of music; compact, economical, swift, of style in language;

profundity, clarity, and so on indefinitely through a thousand familiar epithets, are used to name as well as may be some general character not primarily of structure but of the felt qualitative nature of the whole. And the most resounding and portentous terms, like universality and probability in Aristotle, unity, grace, the monumental in art, accord with the "laws of nature," classic simplicity, and the rest, are of the same sort, sometimes loosely indicating felt structural character, sometimes naming a quality felt at some time by some critic to be the key to all that is fine or great in art.

If the terms used have a disparaging force, they indicate a more or less condemnatory critical evaluation; if the reverse, they indicate praise or approval. That is, they are collectively, in any given case, a slightly more determinate way of saying *good* or *bad*. Obviously we cannot help employing words with such value connotations. But if our criticism is to be informative, if it is to communicate anything relevant to the work of art criticized, the chief emphasis will not be on our own approval or disapproval, but upon precise specifications and indications of kinds of quality. Here it is plain that any term we may employ will communicate nothing absolute, but only degree, with reference to some selected point on a scale of degrees of the quality named. And the zero point of that scale, or the point of maximum or minimum presence of the quality, will have to be defined by the quality as exemplified somewhere in the experience either of other works of art or of events or qualities in nature, and here remembered and applied as a standard.

Compared with Russian novels, for example, English novels are rather mild than intense, whereas compared with one another, English novels vary greatly in emotional intensity, and the term would be positively applicable instead of negatively. The application of this term *intense,* then, amounts to a comparison of the quality of one thing with that of another more or less resembling it in some respect. And in this case it is the comparison of one novel with another, since in other regions of art or experience intensity has the most various meanings. The intensity of sound is a degree of loudness, the intensity of color its brightness or its saturation, depending on our choice of color terms. And there is no distinguishable aspect that is the same in loudness of sound and brightness or saturation of color. In fact loudness in the æsthetic apprehension of sound is an elementary character. From some other point of view than that of æsthetics, that of physics or of physiology, further analysis of this elementary aspect of sound is possible. But for direct discrimination æsthetically, loudness of sound is simply other than brightness and not comparable with it.

Since any intensity actually found as a qualitative aspect of a sense presentation is either such an elementary aspect or the degree of one aspect of a more complex structural qualitative whole, its meaning varies for qualities of structural wholes as clearly as for kinds of elementary æsthetic qualities. And it is not determinate, not *any* aspect of experienced quality, except as limited to a more or less homogeneous range, where minimum intensity is a point on a scale of degrees, below which the applicable term would be whatever names the opposite of intensity, dullness instead of brightness, softness instead of loudness—if, that is, we are to use terms in the way in which criticism does actually employ them. So also of any of the vast number of qualitative terms so common in critical appraisals and so obviously necessary even to description.

An adequate and consistent critical standard of this qualitative sort is then—as in informal ordinary critical usage—simply an indifference point on a scale above which it is positively applicable and below which it is negatively applicable. The ordinary critical vocabulary lacks many of the negatives required for such a scheme; but it at least affords the term *lack* itself. And *lack of* prefixed to the positive term will indicate degrees in the negative direction by further modification. We may say *how* lacking a work is in brilliance or swiftness or steadiness or clarity or intelligibility, by saying that it lacks *all* brilliance, or is *somewhat* lacking in steadiness, and so on. Obviously, none of this has definitely applicable meaning unless we have, marked for us somewhere, the indifference point of the critic's own scale. Critical vocabulary is so extremely inadequate in indicating degrees, in fact, that a perfectly honest review of a very ordinary novel in the critic's own opinion, may make use of adjectives that are equally applicable to novels that the critic himself would rank enormously higher in the very aspects indicated. Constant overt comparison is required to other works of the same author or of other authors to indicate any precise meaning for the terms applied. It is this inadequacy of language to the needs of criticism that makes valuable criticism one of the more difficult literary arts, and never merely a matter of learning names of qualitative standards and their degrees, and designating these in specific cases, any more than it is a matter of applying as criteria recognized structural standards.

But if criticism is single-mindedly engaged on telling us what sort of character specific works of art have, and to what degree they have them, it is plain that the adequately functioning critic will have a whole set of such criteria at his disposal to apply. It is equally plain that the standards cited in the history of criticism, when they are not formal structural characteristics but distinguishable qualitative aspects, are still remembered qualities discerned in other works of art as exhibited in various degrees. The critic's standards, in so far as they consist of such qualitative criteria, will have as adequate a basis as the extent and the depth of his experience has furnished. But they will function to communicate the character of specific works of art to others, only if these others have the same basis to relate them to, unless the critic by various means indicates with some precision his own peculiar qualitative scale, the indifference points at which the degrees of any quality attributed by him positively begin to apply. Except in the very few cases where our adjectives—like those for color and pitch—are systematized pretty fully, the available descriptive terms are so extremely indeterminate that their application alone would hardly differentiate in degrees at all, without explicit comparison. Criticism, as we have it, is too vague in its terminology to be taken very seriously as more than roughly descriptive on the one hand, and on the other as expressive of the critic's personal feeling, and this only to the degree to which his literary powers are adequately creative.

As to final evaluating judgments of the good and the bad in art, it must be clear that these are not in the first place relevant to serious æsthetic appreciation or analysis. The degree of satisfaction actually present in any given case is simply what it is, and an honest judgment will record this satisfaction if a record is asked for. It has long been seen that we call things good because they satisfy us; that we do not—*could* not—learn to desire what is somehow in itself good, since good is necessarily dependent upon individual and social human wants and capacities. Thus serious criticism is never primarily evaluation, but intelligent description and comparison, like all other informative discourse. And the two fairly distinct kinds of standard or criterion used in such discourse are terms naming structural characteristics on the one hand and qualities in varying degree on the other.

One further complication arises here, however. Æsthetic elements are aspects of actual artistic media; specific color and texture appear on a statue because they are the color and texture of particular varieties of marble cut and finished in particular ways. All æsthetic elements and structures occur as of and upon physical media technically employed. Hence most of the clearly intelligible terms in both analysis and criticism refer as definitely to matters of medium and technique as to strictly æsthetic content. The æsthetic content, occurring as it does only upon a medium technically used, used that is in the ways of the arts and of artists, is often most clearly seen and appreciated in its technical functioning. The surest approach to understanding the arts is technical instruction in them, the same instruction that would serve the professional artist, not some supposedly intelligible high-road to appreciation in the very kind of verbal form that blurs the necessary distinctions and passes on to a loose literary account of masterpieces quite unapproachable without the elementary training thus neglected. Even strictly æsthetic analysis cannot avoid the technical aspects of the arts, since by definition an artist's technique is the operation on a medium to the artist's ends, and these ends are clearly enough æsthetic, and so in part define the technical functioning itself in terms of æsthetics.

Thus intelligent technical training is very largely æsthetic, and sound æsthetics is largely technical. To consider training for appreciation radically different from technical training, and to be separately cultivated, is one of the obviously misdirected attempts that helps explain the often total lack of intelligent relation to the arts among civilized people who have had what are called fine opportunities. Learning the structure of the scale in its actual heard nature as intervals in relations, will do more for an appreciation of music than all the lectures in the world, even with musical illustrations drawn from classic works. For the lectures will be devoted to the verbal transfer of intelligent powers of musical apprehension, which is, if not a flat impossibility, at least an apparently hopeless enterprise.

It will be plain, then, that the sketch of æsthetic theory that we have followed through is worse than useless unless it is filled out at every point with the actualities it purports to discuss. Æsthetics itself is theory, not appreciative æsthetic experience; but it is in large part a theory of the nature of the arts, and if it tells us anything at all, it is that such knowledge requires direct acquaintance, since its total subject matter is the qualitative nature of things as presented to us directly through our sensory-affective organic functioning.

INDEX

INDEX

Abstraction, 22, 32; and the intelligible, 42, 55; of pitch, 76; of time, 110; no work of art mere, 139, 146

Accent in verse, 105, 111

Æsthetic content, is not process, 11, 165. *See also* Qualitative

Æsthetic experience, 8, 57, 147, 163; confused with theory, 92

Æsthetic response, 20, 147

Æsthetic surface, 6, 9

Æsthetics, its subject matter, 2, 9, 26, 172, Ch. I; its function, 169; distinguished from the beautiful, 3, 10, 43, from the fine arts, 4, 26, from language, 92, 144, 148, 162, from the practical, 6, 142, from physics and psychology, 10, from the sciences generally, 173, 196; relation to knowledge and science, 11, 20, 25, 30, 39, 111; the science of the immediate, 12; the mathematics of quality, 173; based on the apprehension of structures and orders, 13, 41, 83, 88, 155, 179; task of an adequate, 83; relation to value theory, 178, 187; relation to criticism, 170, Ch. VI; extent of agreement in, 178

Appearance and reality, 194

Apprehension, 13, 41, 83, 88, 155, 179, 188. *See also* Intelligible

Art, conditions of acquaintance with, 15, 26, 159, 166; the good and bad in, 202; as presenting meanings, 164; a common world the object of both art and science, 196; works of, distinguished by the artist's intention, 141, coherence in, 179, individuality of, 187, vagueness of their expression a mistaken notion, 150; conflict of human notions about, 175

Artist, The, his intention, 141, 160; his nature, 28, 161, 168, 184

Balance, misuse of the term, 87

Ballad metre, 130